CHILDREN'S ISSUES, LAWS AND PROGRAMS

SOCIAL POLICY AND SOCIAL CAPITAL: PARENTS AND EXCEPTIONALITY 1974-2007

CHILDREN'S ISSUES, LAWS AND PROGRAMS

Additional books in this series can be found on Nova's website under the Series tab.

Additional E-books in this series can be found on Nova's website under the E-books tab.

DISABILITY AND THE DISABLED – ISSUES, LAWS AND PROGRAMS

Additional books in this series can be found on Nova's website under the Series tab.

Additional E-books in this series can be found on Nova's website under the E-books tab.

CHILDREN'S ISSUES, LAWS AND PROGRAMS

SOCIAL POLICY AND SOCIAL CAPITAL: PARENTS AND EXCEPTIONALITY 1974-2007

DÓRA S. BJARNASON

Nova Science Publishers, Inc.
New York

Copyright © 2010 by Nova Science Publishers, Inc.

All rights reserved. No part of this book may be reproduced, stored in a retrieval system or transmitted in any form or by any means: electronic, electrostatic, magnetic, tape, mechanical photocopying, recording or otherwise without the written permission of the Publisher.

For permission to use material from this book please contact us:
Telephone 631-231-7269; Fax 631-231-8175
Web Site: http://www.novapublishers.com

NOTICE TO THE READER

The Publisher has taken reasonable care in the preparation of this book, but makes no expressed or implied warranty of any kind and assumes no responsibility for any errors or omissions. No liability is assumed for incidental or consequential damages in connection with or arising out of information contained in this book. The Publisher shall not be liable for any special, consequential, or exemplary damages resulting, in whole or in part, from the readers' use of, or reliance upon, this material. Any parts of this book based on government reports are so indicated and copyright is claimed for those parts to the extent applicable to compilations of such works.

Independent verification should be sought for any data, advice or recommendations contained in this book. In addition, no responsibility is assumed by the publisher for any injury and/or damage to persons or property arising from any methods, products, instructions, ideas or otherwise contained in this publication.

This publication is designed to provide accurate and authoritative information with regard to the subject matter covered herein. It is sold with the clear understanding that the Publisher is not engaged in rendering legal or any other professional services. If legal or any other expert assistance is required, the services of a competent person should be sought. FROM A DECLARATION OF PARTICIPANTS JOINTLY ADOPTED BY A COMMITTEE OF THE AMERICAN BAR ASSOCIATION AND A COMMITTEE OF PUBLISHERS.

Additional color graphics may be available in the e-book version of this book.

LIBRARY OF CONGRESS CATALOGING-IN-PUBLICATION DATA
Social policy and social capital : parents and exceptionality, 1974-2007 / editors, Dora Bjarnason.
  p. cm.
Includes index.
ISBN 978-1-61122-758-1 (softcover)
1. Parents of children with disabilities--Iceland. 2. Welfare state--Iceland. 3. Children with disabilities--Government policy--Iceland. 4. Social justice--Iceland. I. Dsra S. Bjarnason.
  HQ759.913.S63 2011
  362.4092'24912--dc22
  2010053458

Published by Nova Science Publishers, Inc. † New York

DEDICATION

This book is dedicated to my son Benedikt, who has taught me so much about love, life and living with disability and impairment. It is also dedicated to my friends Björg and Andrew, and to the memory of Björg's parents, Helga Þorsteinsdóttir and the composer Árni Björnsson. When Björg and I became friends in our youth, her parents welcomed me and introduced me to their ordinary family life with a difference, marked by Helga's heroic resilience after her husband's serious accident, and how she just got on with things, even though no formal support was available at the time to her husband and family.

CONTENTS

Preface		xi
Chapter 1	Introduction	1
	The structure of the book	3
	Vignette 1. The teenage bride in the 1960s	5
	Vignette 2. New millennium: Mary and Peter in the hurricane	7
	Vignette 3. Thor and Helga. A different new millennium	11
	What is a family?	16
	Family life cycles	17
	Disability Studies: a Frame of Reference	18
	Disability studies and social constructionism	18
	Social Capital Theories	19
	Poststructuralistic perspectives	20
	The Purpose of the Study	21
	Key concepts	22

Contents

Chapter 2   History: Milestones of Change   25

    Background   26

    Social Benefits and Public Pensions   26

    Health   27

    Education   29

    Towards Schooling for All?   29

    Special Education   29

    The Current Educational System   31

    Social Affairs and Disability Issues.   34

    The Ministry of Social Affairs   34

    The Disability Legislation   36

    The State Social Security Institute (SSI)   38

    The Regional Offices for the Affairs of Disabled People   40

    The experimental municipal authorities   41

    The State Diagnostic and Counselling Centre (SDCC)   42

    Reflection   43

Chapter 3   Methods and data sources   45

    Access   46

    The sample   47

    The Interviews   50

	Building rapport	50
	The interview	51
	Data analysis, triangulation and checking, and the writing up of findings	52
	Ethical issues	53
Chapter 4	The Older Parents: The Explorers and the Pioneers	55
	The "tragic choice"	55
	The Explorers. From no formal support to a little bit	56
	The Pioneers. Some formal support but not very much	57
	The Struggle	58
	Dealing with Health Care	59
	The birth/diagnosis	60
	Dealing with Assessment	64
	Dealing with the SSI	67
	Dealing with education	69
	Dealing with other services	72
	Parent Advocates	73
Chapter 5.	The Younger Parents: The Settlers and the Citizens of the welfare state	75
	The tragic choice revisited?	75
	The Settlers. Formal support in place?	78

	The Citizens of the welfare state. Great Expectations	78
	Dealing with Health care	80
	Prenatal services	81
	The choice generation	85
	Stories of abortions	90
	Reflections	96
	Dealing with Assessment	97
	Dealing with the SSI	102
	Dealing with Education	104
Chapter 6	The Fathers	109
Chapter 7.	Ordinary Lives with a Difference: Social Capital, Power Games and Parental Reactions	117
	Engaging with social capital	120
	Power games and gate-keepers	124
	Different parental reactions	126
	Conclusion	128
Appendix 1		133
Appendix 2		139
References		157
Index		169

PREFACE

This book is about parents of disabled children, their stories and experiences in a changing world of economic and social policy in Iceland. It is my hope that it will speak to families, researchers and policy makers in and beyond Iceland; that is why it is written in English rather than in my native Icelandic. I owe a debt of gratitude to many people, colleagues, friends and assistants, but most of all to the parents who gave me their stories in the hope that they might inform others, and thus ease the plight of future parents of disabled children. Thanks are due to my friends Dianne and Phil Ferguson at Chapman University in Orange, California, where I started working on the book in the spring of 2009; Dianne spent time with me discussing my findings and the structure of my book. Thanks are also due to Don Cardinal and the welcoming staff at Chapman University. Most of the writing was, however, done in the home of my friends Björg and Andrew Cauthery, during parts of the spring and summer of 2010. Andrew also edited my English. My friend Julie Allan took time out of her busy schedule to read the manuscript, comment on it and give me gentle and constructive criticism, and Helgi Skúli Kjartansson offered comments and corrections on the historical background. The research and data gathering and preliminary analysis took place in the summer terms 2005-2008; I am indebted to my assistants, MA students Hrafnhildur, Ester and Lora who worked with me at different times during those summers and helped with anything from setting up the interviews and transcribing some of them, to answering phone calls. They worked with me on the data analysis, challenged me and added life and colour to my summers. The librarian, Edda Bryndís Ármannsdóttir, provided invaluable help during the final stages of writing. I also want to thank my US publisher Frank Columbus at NOVA for being willing to publish this and my other two

American books. We have never met, only communicated via email; I hope one day we will meet face to face. Finally I want to thank the Icelandic Science Fund (Rannís), the University of Iceland and the former Iceland University of Education for funding this work.

Mardon, Haslemere, UK. 27th July, 2010.

Chapter 1

INTRODUCTION

It is never what happens but the context in which it occurs that gives meaning (Wittgenstein, 1958). This book is about parents of disabled children in Iceland in the period 1974-2007. The book narrates ordinary stories of seventy-five extraordinary families in pursuit of ordinary lives, in a tiny welfare society on an island just beneath the Arctic Circle, as it went through spectacular social and economic changes.

All over the world, families with disabled children experience disability in the family in different ways over time, marked by the *Zeitgeist* and framed by what support is available to them. That is what gives meaning to families' experiences and either opens up or closes off their choices for the future.

The big story from this study is how parents surfed the waves of social policy at different stages of the Icelandic welfare system, constructing their *private problems* as public *issues*. What makes or breaks the surf is the parents' access to and engagement with social capital. There are also smaller, but no less impressive stories of families leading their lives in often taxing situations in pursuit of support for their disabled children and families. Certain themes go through the parents' narratives across time. My findings resonate with other research into parents of disabled children, research done in much larger and more complex societies (Ferguson, Ferguson, and Jones, 1988; Ferguson, 2001a; Ferguson and Ash, 1989; Goodley, 2007; Goodley and Lawthom, 2008; Kirkebæk, Clausen, Storm, and Dyssegaard, 1994; Kristoffersen, 1988; McLaughlin, Goodley, Clavering, and Fisher, 2008).That work suggests similarities in such parents' perspectives and experiences across our societies, despite different socio-economic structures and welfare provisions. Thus this study in Iceland, which can be taken to be a natural laboratory, may help us understand better the plight of parents and exceptionality in modern societies at large.

When I started working on this research in 2005/6, the Icelandic economy was at the height of an economic boom, which in retrospect turned out to be a mirage. There was high optimism for the future of both individuals and society. Iceland was ranked as one of the wealthiest societies in the world, with a well-functioning welfare system available to all. Similarly, education all the way through university was largely financed by the taxpayer. Student loans were in place, and young people could choose one or other of several Icelandic universities or find places at universities around the world. Industry and finance companies were apparently thriving, there was full employment and many foreign workers from EU countries and further afield flocked to the country in search of work.

It was in this climate that I wanted to know more about the experiences of parents with disabled children. Why, in this society of abundance, did parents of disabled children still have to struggle hard for social justice and human rights? Why did parents still have to fight for appropriate education, training, healthcare and social acceptance of their disabled children? What really helped and what hindered their plight, as they pursued their ordinary lives, lives like those enjoyed by their neighbours and friends?

I am no newcomer to disability issues. Since my son, Benedikt, was born in 1980 with significant impairment, I have been a part of that world. We have reaped the benefits of other parents' struggles, and hopefully paved the way for others. In hindsight the changes are spectacular. When Benedikt was diagnosed, just nine months old, I was advised to institutionalise him for both our sakes. I have never been good at following other people's advice if it goes against the grain. So instead, we set out on a fascinating, sometimes challenging journey of learning, travelling, and meeting and making friends and allies (Bjarnason, 2003). My son is now a fully fledged "interdependent adult" (Bjarnason, 2004) leading his life with the support he needs. He is happy, has a home, a job, friends and hobbies and a tiny loving family. This book is a part of that journey. I wanted to know the predicament of other such parents and their children. The welfare system, knowledge, values and resources have been transformed since the 1980s. So why do parents of disabled children still need to fight? What are they fighting for, why and how? What has changed and what remains the same in the parents' experiences?

THE STRUCTURE OF THE BOOK

The book starts with three vignettes portraying very different experiences of parenting a disabled child. The first is a narrative from a mother who had a disabled child in the 1960s when the only services available were the doctor and the institution. The birth of and care for a disabled child in the family were clearly a *private problem*. It also demonstrates how the quality of life of the family improved, as new policies were gradually implemented and values changed. The second and the third vignettes portray two very different stories from the early 21st century, when services were in place but complex to access, and when having a child with disability had become a *public issue* as well as a *private problem*. The second vignette tells the story of a family with a child diagnosed with autism, a complex diagnostic label, living in a regular municipality under the state-run disability service system, and the third vignette portrays a family with a child with Down's syndrome, a less complex diagnostic label, living in one of the new *experimental municipalities*, where local and national services were offered at the community level.

The chapter moves on to ask the question what is *a family*, talks about family life cycles, and how families change and move, and why. Then the chapter outlines the theoretical frame used for the research, disability studies and key concepts, and the purpose of the study.

Chapter 2 deals with the major changes in public disability policy and practice in Iceland, including education, social services and health, over the period 1974-2007. It traces how services have improved and expanded, but also evolved into a complex web of systems, formal rules, services, pensions and grants. Accessing formal support in the late 20th and early 21st centuries could be confusing, as parents attempted to decipher bureaucratic blueprint.

Chapter 3 gives an overview of the research project, its methodology and ethics, and introduces the parents who gave their stories for the book. The families are grouped into four groups: *the Explorers*, *the Pioneers*, *the Settlers* and *the Citizens of the welfare state*, according to the availability of formal support over the period in question. *The Explorers* had next to no formal support. *The Pioneers* set out to create some such supports, *the Settlers* benefited from those, advocated for more and set out to help fill gaps. The fourth group, *the Citizens of the welfare state*, on the other hand, had significant rights and formal support available to them. Because there are no clear cut-off points between the groups, the first two groups will also be referred to as "the older parents", and the latter two groups as "the younger parents" in the text.

Chapter 4 reports some of the findings from the data narrated by the older parents, the *Explorers* and the *Pioneers*. It deals with their choices, experiences and struggles to secure support from family and friends, and formal support from health, assessment, social security, educational and other systems. Their advocacy was instrumental in building a disability lobby, and shaped disability legislation, and other laws, rules and services.

Chapter 5 reports some of the findings from the data narrated by the younger parents, the *Settlers* and the *Citizens* . It deals with similar issues as Chapter 4, but even though the younger parents benefited from their predecessors' struggles, old issues emerged in a different context; new choices, such as whether or not to let a foetus with a difference be born, arose as a result of technological changes in prenatal care. More formal support was added and ordinary schools began to welcome disabled children. Values and lifestyles were also changing. This affected the younger parents of disabled children, their hopes, dreams and expectations, as it did other Icelandic families.

Chapter 6 looks more closely at the fathers' voices. Their perspectives on disability in their families, their roles and tasks overlap with those of the mothers but with a difference. Fathers on the whole try to support their wives even if they do not always agree with them. They have little or no personal support except from their wives, and are less occupied by the labels given to their children. The fathers have concerns about their jobs, interests or hobbies, and some feel stifled by the demands of the family and home.

Chapter 7 considers some of the issues common to all the data. They include everyday life with a difference, parental loneliness, the significance of bonding social capital, and the parents' engagement with bridging and linking social capital, power games and gate-keepers. The chapter finishes with a discussion of different parental reactions vis-à-vis the formal support system.

Chapter 8 is the conclusion. Here I discuss the findings in the light of the questions I brought to the study, and conclude by highlighting what lessons can be learnt from the study by social policy makers, professionals and practice.

This chapter is about the theoretical frame of reference for the study, the key concepts, and its purpose. But we start with three vignettes, the stories of very different families. They all have children with significant impairment, but the children were born into different family and social situations at different times covered by the research.

VIGNETTE 1. THE TEENAGE BRIDE IN THE 1960S

Jón and Sigríður were newly wed, she 17 and he 21, when their daughter, Guðrún, was born with Down's syndrome in the 1960s. They lived in a village on the coast. He was a fisherman and she worked in the village shop. Even though the baby's disability must have been obvious to the medical staff at the birth and to most of the villagers, nobody mentioned this to the parents. They knew nothing about disability, did not recognize the clear signs of her impairment. When Guðrún did not develop at the same rate as other babies, they believed their daughter was a late developer who would catch up in time.

When Guðrún was two years old, she had a minor operation. To the mother's big surprise, a doctor who performed the operation offered to find a permanent place for her. Sigríður did not understand why she got this offer and answered simply "No, thank you", took her daughter and left.

Later, when the little girl was in her fourth year, mother and daughter were out shopping one day when they met a man who mentioned that Guðrún was listed with the local branch of the Association of Parents of Disabled Children. They hurried home without their purchases and went to an elderly aunt, the only female relative nearby, to talk. Later she told her husband what had happened. The child had been labelled. She was an "idiot".

Guðrún became difficult to manage. The parents were exhausted and feared for the safety of their younger children. When Guðrún was eight years old, they were persuaded by their doctor to move her into an institution for people with "mental retardation". The mother described that experience as "the darkest day" of her life and "the hardest thing" she had ever done. Guðrún shared a ward with other children. Her parents tried to keep her in good clothes, but that was hard because all the children's stuff got mixed up, lost or damaged. They visited as often as they could, and Guðrún came home on weekends and holidays. But she lived in the institution, and her parents had no say over what happened there. Her days fell into a routine; breakfast, music, rest, play and walks, each day resembling the previous one. The inmates were seen to be ineducable, so there was no schooling.

Her parents moved to the town where the institution was located and met their daughter almost every day out walking with the other inmates, and, like the others, wearing mismatching clothes and with an unwiped face. This sight hurt. Yet the parents trusted the (largely unskilled) people who took care of their daughter. There seemed to be no other way out.

Times changed. When Guðrún was in her late teens, she and other inmates were moved into a group home for five young people. Although she was not consulted about who she wanted to live with, the move turned out to be successful. Guðrún was no longer locked in or paraded on "institutional walks". She got her own room and her parents could at long last give her things. Sigríður described the day her daughter moved as "a day of shining bright light in contrast to the pitch black darkness" of the years of institutional life.

At the time of the interview, Guðrún was living with five friends from the institution, in a house they had bought with their savings, help from their families and financial support from their municipalities. Staff come in to help, but Guðrún and her housemates shop, cook and clean, dine together some of the time, go out as they see fit, and save up to travel abroad (with a helper) each summer. Guðrún has a part-time job at the local sheltered workshop, but some of her housemates are engaged in ordinary jobs with support. These jobs pay very little, but the tasks are meaningful and need to be performed. Their rights as members of the workforce are limited, and if their earnings rise beyond a small sum per year they will lose a part of their disability pension. They live frugally, and are dependent on their pensions. Sigríður said at the end of the interview:

> I am extremely satisfied. She is in society, a part of this community. She has her own things, her own room, and she looks great. She has become an able potter, can write her own name and is learning to read. She is no longer locked up, denied access to the wider society. I am so very glad, no longer scared what will happen in the future. She is going to be all right.

Then she added:

> I wonder why nobody said anything; nobody gave us information, nobody except my elderly relative was there for us. I was a young woman, strong and cheerful – things had to work out – and they did in the end.

What if…?

The story of Sigríður and her daughter spans the entire period under examination in this book. It highlights how changes in knowledge, welfare state policy and practice impacted her life and that of her daughter. This vignette sets the tone for the book and the lessons learnt.

Sigríður divorced her husband when their children were young and he is not much involved in his daughter's life. When I interviewed her I found a fit, sporty and interesting woman in her sixties, who works full time and devotes her free time to hobbies, sports, her family and friends. But I also found hurt and slight bitterness. Her story captures many of the challenges and the despair experienced by the *Pioneers*, the oldest parents in this study. It also highlights how the lives of many disabled people and their families improved over time. Sigríður's story is one of resilience, struggle and loneliness, but also a story of gratitude for her daughter's adult life and her own adaptability and independence.

VIGNETTE 2. NEW MILLENNIUM: MARY AND PETER IN THE HURRICANE

Kristín is five years old and has been "placed" on the autism spectrum. She is exceptionally beautiful, with curly blond hair and a Mona Lisa smile. She is one of seven siblings and half siblings. Her impairment only becomes obvious when she moves. She is prone to falling, and has several times been to the emergency unit for stitches. She has very little speech but understands more than she can say. Kristín keeps surprising her parents with her unexpected abilities in solving tasks they believed were beyond her. This makes them proud, happy and hopeful.

Mary and Peter met and married in their late thirties. They were both well educated and successful in their working lives, she in technology and he in business. Both had children from previous marriages. They soon had two babies, Peter junior and Kristín. They shared the care for their babies as equally as possible, making what they could of the 9 months of their maternity and paternity leave (Lög um fæðingar- og foreldraorlof nr. 95/2000). But their careers were important, and they soon returned to work, supported by family and hired help.

Nobody Heard...

Mary realized at Kristín's birth that something was amiss. It was a difficult birth, and the baby seemed a bit misshapen, but when she expressed her concerns, she was told not to worry. At the regular four-month post-natal clinic, she voiced her fears again. She was told to take her daughter to a neurologist for tests and consultation, and to a physiotherapist.

Mary discussed her worries with her husband, but was "not sure that he heard" her. Peter realized that his daughter was slow in passing developmental milestones, but the family had stories of "late bloomers".

The waiting for information, for treatment, and to be taken seriously, was agonizing. Mary went from one expert to the next searching for help and explanations. Peter struggled between hope, optimism and acute concern. He found no support except from his wife, but her worries blunted her ability to see his side. They did not see eye to eye, and conflicts were difficult to deal with.

If You Want Something, Make It Happen

Mary's anxiety was intensified by her scientific knowledge; she knew there were unmissable developmental "windows" in a child's early life and that as time passed opportunities were being lost. Eventually, with Kristín now in preschool, they got in touch with the SDCC (the State Diagnostic and Counselling Centre). Pulling strings, they avoided the long waiting list and got Kristín accepted for primary assessment and consultation.

The SDCC gave them some immediate support, explaining their rights and liaising with the preschool to arrange support. As Mary and Peter discovered some six months later, however, the support set up for Kristín fell far short of what it should have been; Mary described it as "a shambles". She battled with the preschool, her local education board and the director of special education. She wrote letters, quoted laws and regulations, demanded explanations, but despite her efforts all the preschool could offer for Kristín's third year was to put her in a class with younger children and without any special support.

The parents were deeply angry and disappointed, but Kristín continued at the preschool for a while because Mary and Peter were pressured at work.

Eight months after their initial visit to the SDCC, Kristín was invited back for a full assessment, a process which lasted a week. She was under observation from a team of experts and underwent a battery of tests. Peter said:

> That is the time when all hell broke loose. It felt as if our lives had been caught in a hurricane...

They faced a new surprise. The label they had been led to believe fitted their daughter's impairment, cerebral palsy, was wrong. The assessment co-ordinator told them that Kristín had to go on a new waiting list to be assessed (by a different department) for autism. The preliminary diagnosis did mean, however, that appropriate rehabilitation and training could get under way.

Reinventing Family Life

Mary soon changed her job in order to direct more of her time and her knowledge to support Kristín. She and Peter devised new routines and rhythms for their everyday lives and faced the fact that they were in this together.

Peter took time off work to pick up Kristín, and to attend courses and meetings. He tried to find time to read up on disability, literature that Mary put his way. Mary organized Kristín's support, kept records, communicated with professionals and the service system. Peter did what he could at home. He spent time with Kristín, and tried to pick up where Mary and the support systems left off. According to Mary, their interaction with the formal system including the SSI (State Social Insurance) and the Regional Disability Office had been satisfactory but at times slow and overly bureaucratic, but at last Kristín was admitted for assessment of autism at the SDCC, and she changed to a new preschool where services were geared to her needs. Experts and therapists were brought in and regular meetings between staff and parents were set up. The parents were happier, they were listened to, taken seriously, and life moved on.

Slowly they learned to trust the people working with Kristín. When the diagnosis finally came, after more than three years of struggle, it turned out to be serious, but less serious than they had feared. Both parents hope that Kristín will continue to be included in school and society with her peers, getting special support, and they expect her to become an active participant in society. Peter still takes the diagnostic labels with a grain of salt. He said:

> Well, something is obviously different with Kristín. These good people who are doing their jobs are not all wrong, but I take things as they come. It would not surprise me if there is a lot more to Kristín than they think.

Peter and Mary are emerging from the hurricane, learning to live with their new existence, gaining strength and trust in their new life and each other. Both ended their interviews with similar thoughts that can be summarized thus: This has been a tough time and it is not over yet, but it has not been pure hardship and no fun. There have been laughter and joy and almost ordinary days. Most of the time we have managed well, and things keep improving.

You get to know the problems, and get used to some of them. We will not run away. We are in this together.

This story shows that there is a complex but highly modern service system available to parents and disabled children. Mary and Peter are urban, upper-middle class, comfortably off and well educated. Their story captures some of the challenges of trying to look after their children while living in the fast lane of their professions; of learning to cope with a child with autism, and a service system that is complex, fragmented and bureaucratic. When confronted by the rules of bureaucracy these parents were not content with joining the queue. Mary's social status, impatience, intellect, and at times lack of diplomacy, have made her a difficult parent to deal with from the professionals' point of view. For some time, Peter's somewhat desperate optimism did not help them to face the system together. In such situations gate-keepers often emerge trying to limit access and protect what they see as their expertise and territory (Lundeby and Tøssebro, 2008a, 2008b). That is part of the explanation as to why the system did not work better. Another explanation may be that despite the sharp and somewhat surprising rise in the number of children diagnosed with autism each year (Dillenburger, Keenan, Doherty, Byrne, and Gallagher, 2010), it is a much disputed and difficult condition to diagnose and controversial as to treatment. Peter and Mary's struggle is in many ways similar to the experiences of several of the older parents, some of whom were described by professionals as "pushy parents" or "parents from hell". These parents (whom I refer to as the *Pioneers*) fought to get services set up to help with their *private problems*. Mary and Peter, on the other hand defined Kristín's needs for services as a *public issue* as well (see Berger, 1963). They knew that services were available and demanded that these should be summoned to help them and their daughter. They defined such help as *a right*. Their child did not, however, fit the clearly defined bureaucratic rules, so Mary used networking and their knowledge to try and bend the rules to secure these *rights*. Thus, like many of the older parents, they were pushing against the system in a way that created resistance, gate-keeping and unnecessary power games. Despite a large social network, informal support was hard to organize, unstable or lacking.

VIGNETTE 3. THOR AND HELGA. A DIFFERENT NEW MILLENNIUM

Daniel (Danni) is a four-year-old with Down's syndrome. When I met him, the sun played in his soft brown hair. He wore a blue overall and a broad smile as he pedalled past on his tricycle, giving an unhappy-looking kitten a ride. He stopped and explained: "Kitty likes…" He lived with his parents and big sister Svala, aged 9, in a modest house on a hill near some farms.

Thor and Helga met in upper-secondary school. Three months later, at the age of 18, they were living together. Just before their graduation Svala was born. The grandmothers helped, and a year later Helga enrolled at university. Thor went to technical college, planned to become an electrician, worked intermittently and is not quite finished yet.

They moved away from their rural community and enjoyed life with their little daughter and lots of new friends. Soon after Helga graduated, they moved back to the country, bought an old house near his father's farm and practically rebuilt it with the help of friends and family. Both found good jobs and life smiled upon them.

Soon Helga became pregnant again with Danni; she had ultrasound scans three times during her pregnancy, the last time because the baby was not positioned right. Other than that everything seemed fine. Danni was delivered by caesarean section at the regional hospital, with Thor present. Helga caught a glance of the baby for just a minute: Danni was blue and was rushed to the neonatal unit. Judging from the faces of the doctor and midwife, Helga suspected that something might be horribly wrong, but she was too frightened and woozy to ask.

Thor recognised immediately that his son had Down's syndrome. He spent the next hours either with their baby or at Helga's side. She cried "as if the world was coming to an end", felt uninformed, inadequate and frightened. For a while she did not want to see the baby. Thor called his mother and mother-in-law and asked them to come. When they and Helga's sister arrived, they too were crying. Thor got irritated, drew them aside and explained: "We have just had a child, not lost one". This worked. They went to see the baby, and Helga's mother returned with a picture of Danni taken by the nurses at the neonatal unit. She said: "He is so wonderful; you have to come up to see him". Helga was eventually taken to meet her newborn.

Thor found the Down's society website, where parents swap stories and pictures. He discovered that "many families seemed to be having lots of fun".

He also phoned an older friend, father of a child with Down's syndrome. This friend explained, listened, and told stories about his family's experience. Thor fondly remembered a girl he had known in his youth who had Down's syndrome. He took heart.

Helga was still crying when a young woman in a t-shirt and jeans entered her room and sat down cross-legged on her bed. At first Helga thought this was a psychologist coming to evaluate her sanity. "I had been crying so hard, that I thought they felt that I was going insane".

The woman turned out to be a paediatrician. Both parents described her as "a brilliant professional". She was clear and precise, heard their questions and answered as an equal. Soon they had good news: Danni did not have a heart condition, and there were no other complications.

Helga and Thor stayed together in the hospital for a week. They talked, cried and they shared the moment when the baby was able to suckle his mother's breast for the first time. Close family and friends came, others phoned or sent text messages with support and congratulations.

The paediatrician proved as good as her word. She sent out information to relevant services. Helga and Thor lived in one of the so called experimental municipalities[1], and within three weeks they were invited to the local developmental therapist (their future service co-ordinator) to plan support and training for Danni. "She called and asked if we wanted her to come to us or if we could come to her", said Helga.

Despite the fact that a child with Down's syndrome had not been born in the community for almost 40 years, things went smoothly. The developmental therapist knew the system, helped fill in forms, provided information on services, organised physiotherapy and more. Danni started in physiotherapy at only 5 weeks old. The midwife came once a week and the developmental therapist (their program co-ordinator)"dropped in like a friend" at least once a week for a while. She gave them her mobile phone number and encouraged them to call if they needed anything.

Helga and Thor valued most of all that their friends and family, their program coordinator and their community stood by them. They also valued highly not having to wait for assessment by the SDCC before receiving local support, which was the rule for parents and disabled children in ordinary municipalities, and could take weeks or even months. Helga and Thor appreciated the help they got from the SDCC staff. They went there together

---

[1] See p. 41. These are municipalities that were permitted to combine community social, educational and local disability services in close co-operation with the centralised health services after a change in the legislation 1996.

on three occasions, first for a short visit and then twice for a week at a time. On the last visit the assessment results were explained to them. For that both their program co-ordinator from back home and Danni's physiotherapist flew to Reykjavík and accompanied them to the meeting. Their trip and expenses were paid for by the municipality.

When describing the people and service at the SDCC Helga said:

> It was good to come there. I have always found everything to do with Danni's support is fantastic. The women at the SDCC are able, good professionals. They knew about Danni before we came, received us well and were helpful. Our local system was working and now it is co-operating with the SDCC.

Before one of the trips to Reykjavík for assessment, Helga fell ill and Thor had to take Danni in by himself. He described that time with fondness: "I was there alone with Danni for 3 days. It was great. I realised how the father is as important as the mother".

Thor was working full time, with overtime some evenings and weekends, for the best part of Danni's first year, while Helga took nine months off from work – six months of their joint parents' leave, and three months she was owed in paid holiday time. In that time she often felt alone, despite her family and friends nearby. She managed her two children and what needed to be done for Danni, went to courses on total communication, and gave him physiotherapy and other training each day. When she finally had to resume her work, Thor took over and used the three months of his parental leave. Helga found it hard to hand over the responsibility, calling him several times a day at first, to ask if he had done this or that. It worried her that Thor, not she herself, was involved in Danni's transition to preschool. Then she relaxed and learnt to trust him. He on the other hand experienced his parental leave as a privilege. He said:

> It is interesting to be able to put your tools away and grab the pots and pans. This, the most important thing in life, the most valuable experience you can have, is to be able to get to know your children.

Since then he has chosen to work a regular 8-hour day with only 1 hour overtime five days a week – most unusual at the time for young men his age and in his line of work.

The preschool worked well. Their program co-ordinator orchestrated the transition. When Danni arrived, they were ready. The staff had been given relevant information and lessons in total communication. One preschool teacher asked to become Danni's support teacher. Danni has become a valued member of his preschool. His parents expect that he will move on to be included in their local compulsory school. They will be able to stay in their community (the nearest special school is in a different part of the country). Svala, the big sister, is happy at school, doing well and has friends.

Helga and Thor were about to get married when I interviewed them. They were optimistic about their future. Helga summed it all up: "I trust in the future, we have learnt so much, and Danni has given us such a lot. I cannot think of life without him".

Helga and Thor live in a rural area which has been given the status of an "experimental municipality" where all public local social and educational services, the state-run health service and services for the support of disabled children are interlinked and locally co-ordinated. Here appropriate formal support is defined as a *public issue* and *a right* by the parents, the professionals and local administrators. Their network of family, friends and neighbours is active and supportive. Furthermore, Down's syndrome is well known and easily detectable, and when, as in Danni's case, there are no serious medical complications, services can be made available without much delay. Contrast their experience with that of Mary and Peter, Kristín's parents. Both Danni and Kristín were born in Iceland in the new millennium. Both families define their and their disabled child's needs as a *right* and as a *public issue* as well as a *private problem*. The difference in the experiences of those two families can on the one hand be attributed to how services were co-ordinated in the *experimental municipality* compared to those in typical municipalities (particularly in the larger urban areas) and to the difference in their children's disability labels. No less importantly, Helga and Thor's social network proved strong enough to support them over time. Their story shows how formal and informal supports can be rallied around a family with a disabled child.

The Three Main Ideas of the Study

The three big ideas I am developing in this study are captured in the vignettes. The first evolves around how social policy regarding health, education and disability impacts the lives, experiences and expectations of different generations of families with disabled children. Peter Berger's ideas about the construction of *private troubles* and *public issues* (Berger, 1963) help unveil the complexities of that and how the parents' meaning-making, their interpretations, expectations and arguments change over time, and why.

As the first vignette demonstrates, the oldest parents had hardly any services available to support them and their disabled child. Gradually new legislation opened up the promise of formal support (see Chapter 2 and Appendix 1), but it took a while for such support to be put in place. Parents of the next two generations found large gaps between what appeared prescribed by law and what formal support was actually available to them and their disabled child in schools, municipalities and from the national safety net. Disability in the family was seen primarily as a *private problem*. Formal support financed by the taxpayers was hoped for, and argued for on a moral basis as if formal support was to be provided out of mercy. The extended family, friends and neighbours were traditionally expected to help.

The two younger groups of parents (especially parents with disabled children born since the mid 1990s into the new millennium) expected services and other formal supports for their disabled children as *a right* and as a *public issue*. This is captured by the second and third vignettes, but in different ways. Many of those parents found themselves disappointed, pushing for generic or specialised services and other formal support, fighting against what they saw as inadequate, rigid, or overly bureaucratic services, benefit structures and professional practice. The discourse seemed to move away from the *private problems* to a *public issue* and a *rights* discourse, and the parents' definitions of their and their children's needs changed. Yet the parents, especially the younger parents, do not speak with one voice.

The second big idea of this study revolves around the parents' access to and engagement with different forms of social capitals (Bourdieu, 1979/1984, 1986; Coleman, 1994; Field, 2003; Putnam, 2000) and how that impacts on the parents' perspectives, actions and well being. Social capital can involve engagement with both the formal support system, shaped via social policy and practice over time, and the informal social capital which is based on our engagement with people in our close network. I believe that social capital can be built around families as well as eroded, and hope the book can throw a beam of light on how that might be done and why it is so important for families with disabled children.

The third big idea concerns the importance of listening to the voices of fathers as well as mothers. Very little research has so far been directed specifically at fathers of disabled children, their experiences and perspectives and what support is available to them as individuals when they have a disabled child in the family (Kirkebæk, et al., 1994). Most such books are written by mothers (Kristoffersen, 1988; O´Connor, 1995; Reid and Button, 1995; Valle, 2009).

However, a few books by fathers exist. Such books by Michael Bérubé about his family's life with his son Jamy inspires many (see for example Bérubé, 1996). Rix, (2003), who had a sister with Down's syndrome brought up in an institution, has a son with the same syndrome, brought up at home and included in his local school. Rix has written candidly about his hopes, dreams and fears for his son. Phil Ferguson also refers to his son's life in many of his writings (Ferguson, 2001). In scholarly work, interviews are conducted either with mothers alone or with parents together, where the mothers' voices come out loud and clear but the fathers' voices much less so (Goodley, 2007). In a previous study I spoke to parents together and discovered that the fathers were largely supportive of the mothers' narratives in the interviews, agreeing with them, adding a few details or correcting facts (Bjarnason, 2004). For this study I decided to talk where possible to the fathers (or partners) individually, and soon realised that their stories differed in significant ways from those of their wives or partners (see Chapter 6).

WHAT IS A FAMILY?

When a baby is born two people become its parents; these are roles that are likely to last for the rest of their lives, however they manage to deal with them. New prenatal technology enabling artificial insemination, the donation of human sperm and egg, surrogate motherhood and more, qualifies that statement, but for most parents it holds true, whether or not the newborn child grows up with his or her blood parents.

There are many different definitions of what is meant by the word family. In a changing global world families come in different sizes and shapes. Sociologists find it increasingly difficult to define the concept of 'family'. Giddens defines a family as "a group of persons directly linked by kin connections, the adult members of which assume responsibility for caring for children" (Giddens, 2001, p. 175). This definition, even though broad, excludes groups of two or more people without children who consider themselves as family. Further people may consider themselves as belonging to the same family without being linked by kin connections. Families in our part of the world can be described as nuclear (married couples or partners with children), married couples or partners without children, one parent families, adoption families, foster families, stepfamilies of different types with one or more cores, gay families, sibling families (one or more generations) and communes. To complicate matters even more, forms of cohabitation of people who consider themselves belonging to the same family vary to a greater extent than ever before. Finally, different forms of experimental cohabitation are also gaining weight. Experimental cohabitation of young people is so common in Iceland that it is considered the norm. Some of these young people stay in the relationship, marry or register their cohabitation, while others return home to their families of origin for a while, or move from one such experimental cohabitation to the next. Social class, ethnicity, different types of religions and religious practices also cut across family types, lifestyles and family values.

Here a family is defined as *a process of interactions* and activities between persons who consider themselves as *belonging* to a particular family. The keywords are process and belonging. No family is static, every family changes through each member's lifecycle, as do the activities, rhythms and routines of the family unit, and the forces that shape these in different families. Gallimore, Weisner and their colleagues, applying ecocultural theory, called these family activity settings and describe them as the *architecture* of everyday life (Bjarnason, 2004; Ferguson, 2001a; Gallimore, Weisner, Kaufman, and Bernheimer, 1989). External factors such as the work and other commitments of individual family members affect the family activity settings in a variety of ways. Ferguson reminds us that "what is important is not so much the activity settings themselves but how a family constructs those and portrays them to others" (Ferguson, 2001a, p. 388). Listening to family narratives of parents of disabled children is thus a key to understanding that particular family.

Family Life Cycles

Figure 1 gives a good illustration of this process for each family that manages to remain intact throughout the couples' lifecycles.

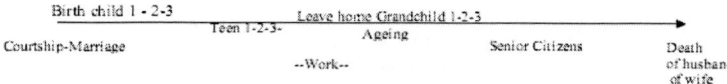

Figure 1. Example of a typical nuclear family life cycle. (In Ferguson, 2001a).

Each point on the continuum takes the family through a variety of activities, tasks and obligations both within the nuclear family, the larger family network, the world of work and other joint and individual activities and obligations. A child with disability is incorporated into the activity settings of everyday family life. Such a child may have different "special needs" at different times and in different arenas, which implies different challenges and different coping mechanisms for the child and his or her family. At the level of family the child needs to be acknowledged, accepted and included, but family activities and the way they are portrayed by family members need to be heard and taken into consideration by professionals working with the child.

DISABILITY STUDIES: A FRAME OF REFERENCE

This study is located within the field of disability studies (Albrecht, Seelman, and Bury, 2001), which views disability as both a socially constructed phenomenon of difference, but also having real consequences for the individual so labelled and for his or her family. The main theoretical frame is social constructionism, but poststructural and social capital theories are also utilized. Social constructionism provides the main theoretical focus to the data analysis, but poststructuralism provides a tool to think about parental roles and reactions in a more critical way, and further helps me look critically at various power dimensions, the parents get entangled within. The social capital theories help my analysis by unravelling and focusing on the importance of trust and engagement with different social networks. What links these approaches is that they are all anchored in and concerned with how humans make meaning out of their lived worlds .

Disability Studies and Social Constructionism

I am interested in "meaning making" in the face of change, including changing policy and practice. The term disability is not a medical model concept, locating a child's difference or disability within the child. As the concept is used here it is a complicated and multidimensional socially constructed concept. A *social relational model of disability* is applied in this study (Bjarnason, 2004; Gabel, 2001; Tøssebro, 2002). From that perspective, "disability" is seen to be a social construct, relational, situational and relative.

Disability studies grow out of a paradigm that rejects the basic epistemology of positivist empiricism that objective facts can be clearly distinguished from values (Ferguson and Ferguson, 1993). Disability studies have a broad and diverse base in the practical experiences of disabled people, and in diverse academic fields such as history, sociology, cultural studies, literature theory, law, public policy, and ethics. Several theoretical stances can be located within a broad social model of disability (Gabel, 2001). What unites disability studies is neither one coherent academic field nor a body of theory, but the claim that the field and its work should be emancipating for and relevant to the practical interests and experiences of disabled people.

The social constructionist position focuses on social processes, inter-subjectivity and interaction (Berger and Luckman, 1967). From the social constructionist perspective we are invited to consider critically the social origins of our taken-for granted assumptions about our perceived reality. Social constructionism does not consist of one unified theoretical approach, but on basic assumptions that create "family resemblance" amongst social constructionists (Gergen, 1994). A social constructionist perspective sharpens the understanding of how the parents in this study perceived their experiences, and how that impacted family activity settings, parents' identities and self images (Ferguson, 2001a). Thus, this lens helps broaden and deepen our understanding of the experiences of parents of disabled children, youth and young adults in times of change in Icelandic society, and hopefully opens up new positive improvements and solutions.

Social Capital Theories

The term "social capital" is useful for understanding the parents' access to and engagement with formal and informal support. I align my use of the term with the work of my colleagues at the AERS Schools and Social Capital Network in Scotland (Allan, Ozga, and Smith, 2009; Bjarnason, 2009a). They base their definition on a literature review of the term social capital and a review of social capital theory. The three people shaping the meaning of the term are Bourdieu (1986), Putnam (1995, 2000) and Coleman (1994) but the AERS scholars draw on wider common denominators of the concept's usage (Allan, et al., 2005). These common denominators include "trust, feelings of belonging and being valued (e.g. shared values) and networks of quality interactions, with a particular emphasis on bridging and linking. Bridging refers to building relationships with a wider, more varied set of people and linking refers to connecting with people who occupy different power positions and have different status" (Campbell, Catts, Gallagher, Livingston, and Smyth, 2005). Bonding social capital refers to engagement with close social networks. The term social capital can amongst other things imply relational behaviour that has emotional perceptual consequences, and it can be taken as an economic metaphor implying a form of power or a resource to be utilised. The level of analysis at which one can put this term to work is micro (the individual in context), mezzo (the organisation or the community) and macro (civic society). This concept helps explore both inclusionary and exclusionary factors at play over time and at different levels within Icelandic society. The concept also helps unravel the structures that make up the formal support systems, and how these legitimate the constructs of the "disabled family", and why (Bjarnason, 2009a).

Poststructuralistic Perspectives

Poststructuralistic perspectives are brought to the study in order to deconstruct meanings, patterns of legitimating principles, and hidden contradictions and dilemmas within the text (Giddens, 1993; Schwandt, 2001). Poststructuralist "arguments" by their very nature attempt to destabilise received conceptions of science, order, society and self. This approach is useful for picking apart and de-prettifying Icelandic social policy, inclusionary rhetoric, and the practice of support. The poststructuralist basic approach is, however, in important ways in direct conflict with the social constructionist approach and disability studies as described above. It is less helpful in giving a voice to individual experience and perspectives. Yet it brings to the study tools for the deconstruction of and critical reflection on the experiences of parents of disabled children over time, and to depict power relations, exclusionary processes and the complexities of the family and the parents' existence.

Foucault (1963/1975) argues that power is situated in social institutions, practices and social relations, and that power and the exercise of power is neither good nor bad but productive and repressive. Power is seen to be exerted through language that produces authoritative and subordinate knowledges. Language is seen as a powerful means of constructing, regulating or disciplining people and places. Power disperses throughout society, through institutions, civil society, and individuals. This approach helps us here to deconstruct the power relations between the parents of disabled children and the professionals they encounter and need for themselves and their children.

Foucault's concept the *gaze* or *the medical gaze* (Foucault, 1963/1975) is useful to open up the practices of medicine and of education as demonstrations of power, both enabling and disabling, producing "special subjects" and "special spaces", encountered by the parents.

THE PURPOSE OF THE STUDY

This book is based on extensive research into how Icelandic parents experienced formal and informal support for their families and disabled child or children over a 33-year time span (1974-2007), a period of significant socio-economic and social policy changes, and how these affect family life and choices.

The overarching question of the study is: Did it become "easier" or "just different" to bring up, care for and educate a disabled child in a time when social disability policy gained weight, and Iceland became gradually more affluent, diverse, global and "messy", and if so why?

The goals of the study are to:

- describe and explore the experience of parents of disabled children and young people of giving birth to and bringing up a disabled child – and their experience of different formal and informal support for the child and the family.
- compare the experiences of parents of disabled children born over a 33-year period (1974-2007); a period of significant changes in law and services aimed at families and disabled children.
- explore whether and in what way there is a connection between the support available and the decisions and choices that parents make on their disabled children's behalf e.g. regarding their placement in segregated or inclusive settings, and even in the late 1990s, with almost universal prenatal scanning of pregnant women, whether or not a foetus identified with a difference should be born.
- explore the positive and negative implications of increased specialization and expansion of formal services directed towards disabled children and their families on their full and active participation in society, and identify in what way specialized and generic support can empower disabled people and their families.

KEY CONCEPTS

Disability

Disability, in this study, is taken to be constructed, embodied and embedded in society and culture. As Gergen (1994) reminds us, social constructionism argues that because we negotiate understandings, and because these understandings can take a wide variety of forms, we can talk of many social constructions of the world. Each different construction brings with it a different kind of action. Particular forms of knowledge in any culture are thus seen to be *social artefacts*.

Following a broad social model of disability (Bjarnason, 2004; Ferguson and Ferguson, 1995) I use the term disability to refer to a social construction, which pushes persons with impairment to the margins of general society. The extent to which this occurs has much to do with relational anchoring and supportive networks and services, social values and attitudes, laws, welfare resources and resource management.

Formal Support

The term "formal support" refers here to all the formal systems and methods that the society has created to help (or control) families and disabled children consequent on "the special needs" that stem from the child's impairment. Formal support includes anything from the first prenatal assessment of the expectant mother and her foetus if it is seen to have a difference, the birth or diagnosis of the child, to health services related to the disability, specialized services in the pre-school, compulsory or upper secondary school, supported work places or holiday camps and other such services. The term also refers to grants and other resources provided by local municipal communities and the state. A considerable body of research in the field of disability studies shows that even a slight hiccup within formal support systems can cause havoc to families with disabled children and young people, reduce the quality of life of all family members and even result in family break-up (Ferguson, 2001a; Turnbull and Turnbull, 1997).

Informal Support

"Informal support" refers to any unpaid help, advice and encouragement provided by extended family members, friends, colleagues and neighbours with the aim of supporting the disabled child or his or her family.

Social Policy and Social Disability Policy

The term "social policy" is here taken to embrace the principles defined by the state and local authorities to govern action directed to improve or support the lives of a given segment of its population seen to be in need of support, together with the systems and practices involved in such actions.

Following Titmuss (1974), this implies actions about *ends* and about *means* to the defined ends. He writes:

> " the concept policy is only meaningful if we (i.e. the actions of government in expressing the general will of the people) believe that we can affect change".

> "To be effective any policy must choose an objective and face dilemmas of choice." (Titmuss, 1974, pp. 23-32).

Social policy should both have defined goals and defined means for reaching those goals. Here inclusive and "special" educational provisions for children with disabilities, public health and social services, assessment services, and the part of the social insurance subsidies intended to support disabled children and their families are all taken to fall under the term social disability policy.

Quality of Life

"Quality of life options" refers to the way people choose to live, how, with whom, and where.

Quality of life also includes access to economic means, opportunities to be with others, autonomy and choice, personal space and opportunity for private life. The extent to which people can access such options provides an indication of the persons' lifestyle, and material and existential quality of life.

Chapter 2

HISTORY: MILESTONES OF CHANGE

How has social policy in Iceland evolved since the mid 1970s to enable most families with disabled children to keep them at home, provide them with care, education and access to society? How has that same policy impacted on the social construct of disabled children and their families; as the "other", objects of pity, diagnosed subjects, or as full, active members of a socially just, diverse society?

Formal support for disabled people and their families has evolved under the auspices of three government ministries: principally the Ministry of Social Services, but also the Ministry of Education and the Ministry of Health. This evolution has not, however, been an entirely coherent process. A vigorous parent movement and disability lobby have been strong instigators of change, but the changing winds of politics, administrative restructuring, new ideas, technology and economic affluence, have all affected where and why formal support has been set up or developed. The implementation of social policy has tended to be piecemeal; new laws have been put in place and existing laws and regulations governing generic welfare services and education have had special clauses added, defining the rights of disabled people and their families. This has sometimes created contradictions between different laws, within the same law and between the laws and relevant statutory regulations, complicating the picture both legally and from the point of view of end users. Furthermore, support has sometimes been centrally administered, sometimes placed under local municipalities.

As support structures developed, many parents found the blueprint for accessing help utterly complex and confusing. A young father interviewed for this study described dealing with bureaucracy as "an additional disability to my family". To ease the reading of this chapter, a chart is included in Appendix 1. It highlights major laws and service provisions as they evolved over the years from 1974-2007. If you are not interested in all the details you are well advised to look at that chart while skimming through these pages.

The period 1974-2007 marks the time when the modern legal framework for health, education, disability and other social services and service systems was put in place or adapted to accommodate disabled people and their families. Professionals with new specialisations (e.g. clinical psychology, special education, developmental therapy, social work and more) emerged and pushed for new or expanded services that would enable them to use their specialised training. This is a time of great change in Iceland, and expansion of its welfare and educational systems.

BACKGROUND

In the 19th century Iceland was a Danish crown dependency and one of the poorest countries in Europe. Its economy was largely based on farming and fishing. In 1880 the population was homogeneous and literate, numbering almost 72,000, over 80% of whom lived in rural areas (Guttormsson, 1983). The country gained independence step by step in the late 19th and early 20th centuries and became a democratic republic in 1944.

The country took a great leap forward in the 20th century to become an urban, highly modern, capitalistic market society; from the 1960s it has ranked as one of the 10-15 most affluent nations within the OECD (Jónsson, 2009). Much, however, has changed since the financial collapse of 2008, and the effect this will have on Icelandic society in the long run remains to be seen (Jóhannesson, 2009). One thing is clear. The economy and welfare services are being scaled down as I write. The full impact of these cuts will not be known for some time, but they will hit hard. This includes formal support for families of disabled children.

SOCIAL BENEFITS AND PUBLIC PENSIONS

In 1936 a comprehensive general public insurance law was created (Lög um alþýðutryggingar nr. 26/1936) to combine all existing insurance and public benefits that could secure and support every Icelandic citizen from birth to death. Sick benefits were mentioned in the law, but there were administered by health-benefit cooperatives (sjúkrasamlög) under local communities. The legislation marked the beginning of the SSI (State Social Security Institute). Ólafsson (1999) points out that frugality in public spending, especially for social support and benefits to the general public, was a paramount concern of the state in the early and middle 20th century. In people's minds there was also, for much of the 20th century, a stigma attached to receiving benefits, and the new social support systems were designed in a way that took informal support by family and friends for granted (Alþingistíðindi, 1992).

Ólafsson argues that:

> On the whole one can state that the element of self-help is larger in the Icelandic welfare system than in the other Nordic countries. The redistributative effects of the Icelandic system are also less effective than those of the other Nordic systems, resulting in slightly higher levels of poverty amongst pensioners and the general population of Iceland (Ólafsson and Jónsson, 1991p.31).

This also applies to invalidity benefit pension and much social service provision for persons with disability and their families (Herbertsson, 2005; Ólafsson, 2005).

HEALTH

Public health services are run and organized directly by the state, under the Ministry of Health, which controls public health and preventive health services, local health centres, hospitals and other health related organizations; health services in nursing homes, rehabilitation and treatment centres, medicine and medical technology, and professional credentials within the health system (Ministry of Health, e.d.)

Between 1969 and 2008 the remit of the Ministry (then titled Ministry of Health and Social Security) included also the administration of social security. Since 2008 the new Ministry of social affairs and social security (Félags- og tryggingamálaráðuneytið, 2008) has taken over responsibility for social security, though the Ministry of Health continues to handle sickness and accident benefits and sickness pensions (Reglugerð um Stjórnarráð Íslands nr. 177/2007). Much of the general public health service is provided at minimum or no cost to the individual patient [1]. Funding comes largely from the state through taxes (Lög um heilbrigðisþjónustu nr. 40/2007).

Specialist treatment in Reykjavík and the other more densely populated areas is provided largely by private medical specialists working under contract to the SSI (State Social Security Institute); they also visit health centres in the less densely populated areas of the country. In addition, outpatient specialist services are provided by the hospitals. No referral is required for specialist treatment (Heilbrigðisráðuneytið, e.d.).

There are three types of hospitals: 1) specialised hospitals, the National University Hospital in Reykjavík providing highly specialised hospital service for all people in Iceland, and general care for the residents of the capital city area; and the teaching hospital in Akureyri, 2) regional hospitals with a certain degree of specialisation, and 3) local hospitals. Many local hospitals also function as old people's homes and nursing homes. Other health institutions include rehabilitation hospitals and clinics for substance abusers (Heilbrigðisráðuneytið, e.d.).

Physiotherapy is partly provided in health centres, but mostly by privately practising physiotherapists in the urban areas, working under contract to the SSI (NOMESCO, 2008). Dentistry is largely paid for by the patient, but costs are subsidized or even paid in full by the state (through the SSI) to pensioners, children and disabled people (Tryggingastofnun ríkisins, e.d.a).

The infant mortality rate in Iceland is one of the lowest in the world and longevity one of the highest. Both prenatal and postnatal services are close to state of the art (Heilbrigðisráðuneytið, e.d.). Most children are born in hospitals (Bjarnadóttir, Garðarsdóttir, Smárason, and Pálsson, 2008), and neonatal services provide home aftercare. Home visits are made 3-5 times in the first two months, by midwives or paediatric nurses. The baby is weighed and measured on each visit. Subsequently the baby is brought to the local hospital or health centre for medical checks at 6 weeks and again for immunization injections, the first one at three months. At the ages of three and a half and five years, the child attends for sight, hearing and development tests (Heilsugæsla höfuðborgarsvæðisins, e.d.).

Ultrasound technology was introduced in 1975, and by 1986 all pregnant women in Iceland had the option of a free prenatal ultrasound scan in the 18th or 19th week of pregnancy (Landlæknisembættið, 2008). Ultrasound is fast

---

[1] Health centres are responsible for primary health services, including preventive services and general medical treatment. Preventive services include child health care, maternity care, school health care, immunization, family planning etc. Home nursing care is also the responsibility of the health centers.

becoming an integral part of every pregnancy (Geirsson, 2001): by 2004 approximately 99% of all pregnant women in Iceland availed themselves of this option. At that time approximately 80% of all pregnant women in Iceland also went for an earlier scan, for a small fee, in the 11th to 14th weeks of pregnancy. That number is now approaching 90%. When impairment is suspected a subsequent battery of tests (e.g. blood tests and maternal serum tests) is carried out (Bjarnadóttir, et al., 2008).

The Ministry of Health wields the largest part of the National Budget each year. It has almost all Icelandic health workers on its payroll, in addition to operating and maintaining health related organisations, technology and medicines, and the above mentioned sickness and accident pensions and benefits (Hagstofa Íslands, e.d.a; Ministry of Health, e.d.)

EDUCATION

Towards Schooling for All?

In the 1960s and early 1970s most parents who kept their disabled children at home did not have the opportunity of sending them to school. Some parents, especially parents of children labelled intellectually disabled, sent them to live at one of the relatively new institutions for care and possibly some training. Most professional experts of the time recommended this, especially if they were seen to have severe intellectual or multiple impairments, but a few parents and professionals had a different idea (Bjarnason, 2004; Jónasson, 2008).

SPECIAL EDUCATION

A few institutions for people with intellectual impairment were established, the first in 1930, but mostly in the 1950s and 1960s. From the beginning, institutions provided some training and even formalized instruction to inmates considered able to benefit from it. Certain groups of disabled children, e.g., the blind and the deaf, enjoyed some education from the late 19th century onwards (Sigurðsson, 1993).

In 1961, Höfðaskóli in Reykjavik opened for school-aged children with IQs between 50 and 75 who lived at home, and in 1969, a boarding school opened for a few years for children with physical disabilities (Jónasson, 2008; Sigurðsson, 1993). Most disabled children living at home, however, had little or no access to formal schooling until long after the 1974 Compulsory School Act. Learners with "special educational needs" due to poverty or other social problems were provided with some educational support, often in segregated settings, in the 1950s and 1960s, and institutions for "problem children" were established (Forsætisráðuneytið, 2008).

In 1974 Höfðaskóli was replaced by the special school Öskjuhlíðarskóli in Reykjavik for learners with IQs between 50 and 75 "Reglugerð um sérkennslu nr. 270, 1977). This school is still in operation. Children labelled with physical disabilities were in 1975 moved from the boarding school into a special class in the nearby general education school, Hlíðaskóli. Many of those students were soon integrated partially or fully into typical classes. This marked the beginning of "integration" or "mainstreaming" in Icelandic schools; that is placing students on a continuum from typical classes to segregated special classes or special schools on the basis of severity of their impairment and assessed needs (Jónasson, 2008; Sigurðsson, 1993).

New professionals and therapists of various kinds, certified to work with disabled learners, appeared in schools. The special educators and other professionals brought new methods and new visions from their studies abroad, and education of disabled and other learners with special needs began to evolve. The professional focus was primarily on diagnostic skills and systematic teaching and training methods aimed at reducing the learners' problems stemming from their impairment (Bjarnason and Persson, 2007; Jónasson, 2008).

In 1977, the first statutory regulation was set for special education, establishing a framework for special education services at the compulsory school level (Reglugerð um sérkennslu nr. 270/1977). The regulations prescribed different special schools and special classes based on learners' IQ scores and disability labels. In 1980, students classified as severely and profoundly disabled and who lived at home could at last attend school. Safamýrarskóli, a special school for severely and profoundly disabled children (IQ below 50), opened that year, gathering such children from all of Iceland (Sigurðsson, 1993).

Special classes also began to appear in general education schools, particularly in the urban areas in the south west, and a special school for children with intellectual impairment was established in Akureyri, a town in the north. Psychological and guidance services became part of the general school system, and services for so-called slow learners and students with particular learning problems became more firmly established (Jónasson, 2008).

The first special educators studied abroad; mostly in Norway and the other Scandinavian countries. In the 1980s and 1990s, special education undergraduate courses were developed at the Iceland University of Education (IUE). Soon, teachers were invited into a BA. program and later MA. and MEd. programs at the Department of Special Education at IUE (Bjarnason and Persson, 2007). Since 2006 PhD. programs have opened at the Iceland University of Education, now The School of Education at the University of Iceland, after a merger of the two universities in 2008.

In the 1990s most of the institutions and special schools were closed down under the influence of the inclusion movement, but there are some signs that may be changing (Bjarnason, in print; Þorláksson, Hjaltason, and Sigurðardóttir, 2008).

THE CURRENT EDUCATIONAL SYSTEM

The framework for the current educational system was established by comprehensive compulsory education legislation introduced in 1974 (Bjarnason and Persson, 2007; Edelstein, 1988; Guttormsson, 2008). That legislation did not apply to preschools. The legislation prescribed different types of special schools for disabled learners, depending on their IQ levels (Jónasson, 2008; Reglugerð um sérkennslu nr. 270/1977).

Preschool

Preschool for children aged 1-6, though part of the educational system, is not compulsory, and parents pay a subsidized fee. The preschool system developed from day-care for disadvantaged children (in 1924) to a comprehensive system of playschools and day-care establishments under the Ministry of Education from 1973 (Lög um hlutdeild ríkisins í byggingu og rekstri dagvistunarheimila nr. 29/1973).The preschools were (and still are) run by local communities but in the 1990's, they became (a non compulsory) part of the school system.

In 1994 a law was passed incorporating all preschools into the primary level of the state educational system (Lög um leikskóla nr. 78/1994). Currently approximately 40% of children aged 0-2, and almost all aged 3-5, attend preschool. In the 1980s a couple of special classes were established for disabled children at preschool level but they were closed in the following decade. Now all disabled preschoolers are entitled to have appropriate special education services in general preschools (Lög um leikskóla nr. 78/1994, nr. 90/2008).

Compulsory Education

Compulsory education is mandatory for 10 years from the age of 6 to 16. It was a centralised system under the Ministry of Education and Culture until the mid 1990s, when a law was passed separating state and local community services (Lög um breytta verkaskiptingu ríkis og sveitarfélaga, nr. 87/1989; Lög um félagsþjónustu sveitarfélaga nr. 40/1991). Now compulsory education is under the municipalities but overseen and evaluated by the Ministry (Lög um breyting á lögum um grunnskóla nr. 66,1995, nr. 77/1996 ; Lög um grunnskóla nr. 49/1991; Lög um grunnskóla nr. 91/2008).

The compulsory education system is funded by the taxpayer, and free of charge to students and their families (Ministry of Education, Science and Culture, 2002). Since the 1990s, special classes have been operated for students with intellectual and multiple disability labels. Currently between 15% and 20% of all compulsory school students in Iceland get some special education support in ordinary schools and classes, and 0.4% in special schools (Morthens, 2009).

The Reykjavík School Board decided in 2000 to focus on inclusive education, closing down its special classes and providing special support in classrooms or resource rooms (Fræðsluráð Reykjavíkur, 2002). Outside the Reykjavik area, local education authorities mostly also support students with special learning needs inside regular schools and classes. This is done both to keep the families in residence, and because there are relatively few students with significant (and expensive) needs in each of these smaller areas, making special schools and special classes not economically viable. Extra cost for such support is paid by a special government fund (Reglugerð um jöfnunarframlög Jöfnunarsjóðs sveitarfélaga til reksturs grunnskóla nr. 351/2002).

Upper Secondary Education

The upper-secondary school system is also largely free of charge for the students. It is still administered directly by the Ministry of Education (Ministry of Education, Science and Culture, 2002). Well over 90% of all compulsory school graduates enter the upper-secondary system, but the dropout rate is high (30% - 40%). More boys than girls drop out, though some return to school some years later for vocational or technical education (Jónasson, 2008). The 1988 Upper-Secondary School legislation declared for the first time that these schools were for everyone. In 2008 new legislation was passed (Lög um framhaldsskóla nr. 92/2008) prescribing an expansion of upper-secondary educational programs with special classes or units tailored to the needs of disabled young people.

The first special classes in upper-secondary schools began to emerge in the mid and late 1990s and were certified by law in 1996 (Lög um framhaldsskóla nr. 80/1996). At first the special classes were a two-year option, but by 2001 disabled students were enabled to attend the schools for four years. Some of those special classes gradually opened up, enabling disabled students to mingle with the regular student body, and a few of the disabled students were supported to attend some regular classes. Most of the upper-secondary schools fully include non-labelled students identified as having special educational needs, and many partially include disabled students from the special classes or units (Gísladóttir, 2007; Ragnarsdóttir, 2005).

There are still, however, traditional grammar schools (they see themselves as elite schools) which do not have special classes and do not welcome students with "special educational needs" or intellectual impairment.

Even upper-secondary schools that accept disabled students into special units or classes, can select from amongst disabled applicants whom they admit or reject. Principals of these schools are entitled to do this, as different schools specialise in serving disabled students with different labels and diagnosed special needs (Lög um framhaldsskóla nr. 92/2008). From the disabled students' and their parents' point of view this rule complicates matters greatly, because disabled students may be faced with only one option when selecting an upper-secondary school.

Post-Upper-Secondary Education

Post-upper-secondary education is largely closed to students with intellectual impairment. One small school, Fjölmennt, takes on some of those students for short courses, and the University of Iceland School of Education has pioneered a university program for a small group of students with intellectual impairment who want to work as assistants in educational and youth facilities. This, a two year program, is now in its third year and is immensely promising.

Most people with significant impairment attend either sheltered workshops or resource centres, but disabled adults have also begun to find work through supported work programs in the regular labour market.

The Salamanca Declaration

In 1994, Iceland became one of 92 states and some 25 international organisations to sign the Salamanca declaration (United Nations, 1994).[2] Since then inclusive education has become the law at all school levels except for university level.

Despite this, four special schools and several special classes in regular schools are still operated at the compulsory level. The current compulsory educational legislation (Lög um grunnskóla nr. 91/2008) is the first to mention the words "inclusive education" in the legal text, and then only in article 17 dealing with "special needs" education.

SOCIAL AFFAIRS AND DISABILITY ISSUES

The Ministry of Social Affairs

The division of responsibilities between the Icelandic ministries is complicated to say the least.[3] As mentioned earlier (under 'Health'), sickness

---

[2] Iceland has signed several international treaties and declarations concerning the importance of education and the right of all children to get educated. Thus Iceland has signed the UN declaration of Human rights (1948) The European Declaration of Human Rights (1950), The UN declaration of the Rights of the Child (1992), the UNESCO treaty on Economic, Social and Human Rights (1979), the Salamanca declaration (1994), and the UN treaty on the rights of disabled people (2007). These declarations and treaties have in common that they all declare the equal right of all individuals to education.

[3] See Appendix 1. The chart shows clearly how the division is made especially complicated regarding support for disabled people between the Ministry of Social Affairs and the Ministry of Health, as the line between social and health issues in real life is blurred yet the two matters interconnected in nature. In addition to the blurred and constantly changing responsibilities numerous agencies operated under the ministries serve to make it harder for the average citizen to understand. The latest changes and restructuring of the Ministry of Social Affaires; now the Ministry of Social Affairs and Social Security from 2008

pensions and other benefits are administered by the Ministry of Health, but responsibility for the complex system of support for disabled people and their families is borne by the Ministry of Social Affairs and Social Security, firstly through the provisions of the Law on the Affairs of the Disabled (Lög um málefni fatlaðra nr. 59/1992) which declares the aim of enabling people with disability and their families to lead as normal lives as possible within society; and secondly via the law on SSI (The State Social Security Institute), an organization that provides insurance coverage to the population (Lög um almannatryggingar nr. 117/1993). These two main official bodies for support will be described in more detail below.

Until 2008 the Ministry was structured into three professional departments; Welfare, Social Security, and Equality and Labour. The responsibilities of each department are shown in the table below:

Responsibilities of the Ministry of Social Affairs and Social Services 2007

Department of Welfare	Department of Social Security	Depart. of Equality and Labour
Children	Pensions and State Social Assistance Benefits	Equality
Disabled Persons		Immigrants
Family Affairs	Maternity/paternity and Parental Leave Benefits	Employment
The Elderly		Occupational Health and Safety
Local Authorities ' Social Service	Unemployment benefits	
Housing	Chronically Ill children	
Principal Tasks		
Department of Welfare	Department of Social Security	Department of Equality and Labour
Preparatory work on policy	Pensions and State Social Assistance Benefits (invalidity benefits)	Preparatory work on policy
Consultation and contact with interested parties		Consultation and contact with interested parties
Consultation and professional supervision of state bodies	Consultation and contacts with interested parties	Consultation and professional supervision of state bodies
The Disabled persons Construction Fund	Consultation and professional supervision of state bodies	International relations
The Senior Citizens' Building Fund	Rulings and opinions	Rulings and opinions
International relations	Professional advice to the Minister on the above issues	Professional advice to the Minister on the above issues
Rulings and opinions		
Professional advice to the Minister on the above issues		

(Félags- og tryggingamálaráðuneytið, e.d.a).

It was the intention to devolve services for disabled people from the Ministry to local communities by 2010, but this plan appears to have been moved forward to 2011 due to the economic uncertainty in Iceland (Félags- og tryggingamálaráðuneytið, e.d.c).

The Disability Legislation

The current law is initially based on the 1979 law on *Assistance to the "Mentally Retarded"* (Lög um aðstoð við þroskahefta nr. 47/1979) which marked the beginning of community support services for persons with disability. Under this legislation the Board of Administration for Assistance to the "Mentally Retarded" was established. Subsequent legislation refers to Regional Boards for the Affairs of People with Disabilities, serving the eight service regions defined in the 1979 Act for individuals with intellectual disability. In 1983 the law was extended to apply to people with physical and sensory impairment, as well as those labelled with intellectual disabilities. Subsequently in 1992 this was further extended to include people with chronic mental illness.

The 1979 law declared the right of people with intellectual impairments to lead as normal a life as possible. Although the current 1992 law on the Affairs of the Disabled now applies to a much broader group of disabled people, the main goal, and the administrative structure, has remained for the most part the same since 1979 (see however p. 41, the *experimental municipalities*). According to the 1992 law, the first paragraph states:

> The aim of this law is to secure disabled people equal rights and a comparable quality of life to that of other citizens, and to create for them opportunities to lead a normal life. .. (Lög um málefni fatlaðra nr. 59/1992, paragraph 1).

This paragraph, the spirit of the law, raises important questions, such as what is meant by "equal rights", "comparable quality of life", and "opportunities to lead a normal life"?[4]

---

[4] In the white paper accompanying the Bill, heavy emphasis is placed on the rights of disabled people to make use of generic services especially health, education and social services. The white paper emphasises that a special effort should always be made to serve people with disabilities according to generic legislation. It is further proposed that a special comity based on the co-operation of the three ministries involved (Ministry of Social Services, the Ministry of Education and Culture, and the Ministry of Health and Public Insurance as it was called then) and representatives from the major interest groups of disabled people should be established to oversee the procedures.

The reference group "other citizens" is also problematic. Citizens lead a variety of lifestyles; have different life choices and means to achieve them. I take the stated goal in the law to refer to what is generally seen as acceptable in terms of material and existential quality of life, anchored in human rights.

The law defines who is entitled to support and services under the law thus:

> The right to services under this law is assigned to each person who is mentally or physically disabled and needs special services for that reason. The law applies to people who are intellectually disabled, mentally disabled, physically disabled, disabled due to lack of sight or hearing. Furthermore, disability can result from chronic illness or accidents (Lög um málefni fatlaðra nr. 59/1992, paragraph 2).

This clause is also somewhat unclear. The remaining paragraphs in the disability legislation define the administrative structure of special service provisions, the special rights [rights additional to those of general citizens] that disabled people are entitled to under the law, and the means made available to reach the prescribed ends. Despite the fact that this law has been amended several times, the above clauses have not changed.

Each year, the Budget and the Treasury determine the real amount of money the state and municipal authorities (until 1994) allocate to these and other welfare services. According to the 1992 Act (with subsequent amendments), the state and some local communities[5] (referred to as *experimental municipalities*) are ultimately responsible for the provision of services, monitoring them and ensuring quality control and accountability.

The 1992 law as amended defines and prescribes the rights of disabled people to support and services beyond generic legislation. These include family support, the provision of specialised equipment such as wheelchairs and walking aids, assessment services, respite, support at home, special medical and to some extent special educational provisions, and more. Some of these services and supports were already provided in the previous legislation, others were new. The overarching goal of the 1992 law remained that of normalization and inclusion of disabled people with other citizens in generic

---

Further it is stated that: "The right of disabled people to enjoy generic services is fundamental to their human rights. The goal of the law regarding equal rights and comparable quality of life to that of other citizens will not be reached unless this fundamental principle is respected (Alþingistíðindi, 1991). From this it is clear that the law is intended to foster integrative services and an inclusive society.

[5] These were the municipalities of Akureyri and the Westmann Islands 1994. Later three more municipalities took on similar services.

public services and society. And yet the disability legislation has given rise to more segregated special services than any other legislation in our history.

The State Social Security Institute (SSI)

The SSI is the central state welfare agency with the role of distributing State grants, pensions and benefits. Social security is financed by the State Treasury. Everyone who has been legally resident in Iceland for a certain period of time automatically becomes a member of the Icelandic social security insurance system, regardless of nationality. Entitlement is, however, subject to conditions, for example regarding age, disability, length of residence, income and family circumstances.

The SSI has administered the social protection system since 1936 (Lög um alþýðutryggingar nr. 26/1936). Since that time there have been several changes to the legal framework, and the system has gradually broadened its scope. In 1970 the SSI became the responsibility of the new Ministry of Health and Social Security; under new comprehensive legislation on public insurance (Lög um almannatryggingar nr. 67/1971), parents of children with disability, aged 1- 6, could for the first time claim a small grant towards the care of their disabled child, and in 1986 a centre for the provision of mechanical aids such as wheelchairs for disabled people was established under the SSI. Despite legislators' attempts to restructure and economize, the system has expanded steadily; by 1997 SSI expenditure was 22.8% of the total national budget, and its outgoings doubled in value between 1998 and 2006, largely due to higher numbers of old age and invalid pensions coupled with an increase in the amounts paid out in benefits per person (Herbertsson, 2005).

Following the 2007 Social Security Act (Lög um almannatryggingar nr.100/ 2007) responsibility for all social security issues except those directly related to public health and health issues was moved to the Ministry of Social Affairs and Social Security; prior to that, the public insurance system was divided into three sections; Pension insurance, Health insurance[6], and Occupational injury insurance (Lög um almannatryggingar nr. 117/1993), and this was the social security structure within which most of the parents interviewed for this study operated.

---

[6] Health insurance was moved from The Ministry of Social Affairs to the Ministry of Health by 2008.

The SSI administers social assistance from the State (except, since 2008, health related insurance), but family benefits (child allowance) are administered by the Directorate of Internal Revenue (Tryggingastofnun ríkisins, e.d.a); the SSI also serves as a clearing house for paying out the various benefits that families and disabled children are entitled to under Disability, Health and other legislation.

The SSI pays out grants to parents of disabled children for "family care and extra expenses due to chronically sick or disabled children" based on medical evaluation of the level of care needed[7] and paid according to a "laundry list" of estimated severity of diagnosed disability labels[8]. Such grants are reduced or removed when special services such as respite care or institutionalisation are provided, or when a child becomes more able to take care of him/herself. Over time new grants and benefits have been added and others have gradually become more generous, until 2009 when they were pruned. New technology has made possible things such as the adaptation of cars for people with mobility problems or computer controls for children in wheelchairs. Users are, however, expected to pay part of the costs unless they live on invalidity pension alone.

---

[7] Payment for family care and extra expenses due to disabled or chronically sick children: Group 1.Children who due to very significant impairment/ multihandicap are completely dependent upon others for mobility and/or most every day activities. Group 2. Children who due to significant impairment are in need of support and almost continuous supervision in their everyday life. For example children with significant to medium severe mental retardation, physical impairment and in need of a wheelchair, severe problems with making contact, autism, deafness and use of sign language or lip-reading, and blindness. Group. 3. Children who need support and supervision every day. For example because of moderate mental retardation, mobility problems and in need of splints or crutches for mobility, hearing impaired children who need a hearing aid for both ears, children with significant loss of sight in both eyes. Group 4. Children with developmental or behaviour problems comparable to disability or mental illness, who need training and observation by specialists and support in school, at home and with peers. Group 5. Children with moderate developmental or behaviour problems, who need training and observation by specialists (Tryggingastofnun ríkisins, e.d.b).

[8] Parents of children that fit the disability groups 1-4 described above (in footnote 7) receive a grant for care and additional expenses due to the child's impairment of from 106,912 kr. (approx. 850 euros) per child diagnosed as 100% impaired to 26,728 kr. (approx. 212 euros) for a child diagnosed with 25% impairment each month. Children diagnosed under category 5 did not warrant such a grant. The figures are from 2008. The diagnosis must be confirmed and registered by the State Diagnostic and Counselling Centre, the Icelandic Institution for Sight Impairment, and the Hearing Impairment and Deaf Centre of Iceland (Tryggingastofnun ríkisins, e.d.c). These figures are from before the economic crash and the drop in the value of the Icelandic kr. These payments (in Icelandic kr. 2009) have in 2010 been cut by around 18% (Sigurðsson, 2010).

The SSI provides a number of specific grants for disabled children and adults (such as grants towards adapting a home for the use of a person in a wheelchair, or for car purchase for those with significant mobility problems) and it foots most of the bill for health services, physiotherapy, dentistry and more. In the case where a child with disability or serious illness has to go abroad for a lifesaving operation, this is paid for by the SSI together with a total or partial travel grant for an accompanying parent. Any such case involves a complex application process to establish what rights the child and family have.

The Regional Offices for the Affairs of Disabled People

Ever since the 1979 law on Assistance to the "Mentally Retarded", the country has been divided into service regions for the purpose of administering the affairs of people with disabilities.

Some of the service regions were later divided into special service areas, based on local municipalities, local regional boards or co-owned agencies of the municipalities. This came about following the 1994 legislation relating to experimental municipalities; under the previous law, each service region has a Regional Board for the Affairs of People with Disabilities, but the experimental municipalities were provided with a different administrative structure, as described below.

The main tasks of the Regional Boards are to ensure that local disability services are in accordance with the objectives of the Disability Act (1992); to advise the Minister of Social Services on regional matters; to co-ordinate and administer local disability services; and to oversee the rights of people with disabilities and ensure that they receive the services they are entitled to (Lög um málefni fatlaðra nr. 59/1992).

Each Regional Board consists of seven people, a local representative for health, social services, three representatives from local organizations, one of whom should be the director of local social services, two representatives of consumer groups, and a representative appointed by the Minister. A representative of the local school board, though not a member of the Board, has to be consulted on school matters (Lög um málefni fatlaðra nr. 59/1992, paragraph 6).

Each region has a regional office, whose role is somewhat confusing; on the one hand these offices administer local services to disabled people, working within a tight budget; on the other hand they are expected to secure rights and provide advocacy support (Lög um málefni fatlaðra nr. 59/1992). This invites the possibility that the advocacy and support roles play second fiddle to the role of distributing limited sums of money to pay for services.

The Experimental Municipal Authorities

In 1990 a new law came into force separating responsibilities between the state and local authorities (Lög um breytta verkaskiptingu ríkis og sveitarfélaga, nr. 87/1989). The intention of this diversification was to reduce the number of centralized services (education, health, social services, services for the aged and so forth) and to clarify payment responsibilities. At the same time it was argued that local communities were closer to the people and could provide more cost-effective and possibly more appropriate services than a centralized state apparatus. In 1994 a law was passed to enable a few local municipal authorities to experiment by devolving certain services from the state to the communities (Lög um reynslusveitarfélög nr. 82/1994). At first (1996) two municipal authorities took on the affairs of people with disabilities – Akureyri (the main town in northern Iceland) and the Westmann Islands. They joined or opened up co-operation between domains of responsibility, such as the local social services, the local preschool and school administration, special services for disabled people, local child protection services and health services. Since 1996 more local authorities have taken on this challenge. In 2008 five local communities provided such services for disabled people and their families (Félags- og tryggingamálaráðuneytið, e.d.b).

The state foots the bill to a large extent, but increased flexibility in the application of municipality funds is supposedly in place. As a professional working within such system explained:

> "Now the systems can work and talk together. Before, each department was sworn to secrecy in matters concerning their work. There were bureaucratic walls ... Now we get information about the disabled child from the health system as soon as the child is born or even before, and we also know about other needs of the family. Now we can work with the schools, social service support, child care authorities and the State Diagnostic and Counselling Centre. This makes it so much easier for us to support families when they need it and wish for help".

Most parents interviewed who lived in the experimental municipalities and chose to use available support were pleased. The advantage, from their perspective, was that a single professional person came, offered help, co-ordinated services, and stayed in contact with the family over the long term, from birth right through a disabled child's schooling.

The State Diagnostic and Counselling Centre (SDCC)

The State Diagnostic and Counselling Centre (SDCC) is the main assesment and habilitation centre in Iceland for children and young people believed to have developmental difference. The Centre opened in 1986; prior to this, a similar service had been provided by the Kjarvalshús Assessment Centre, operating as a department of the Öskjuhlíðarskóli State Special School (Jónasson, 2008).

Administered and funded by the Ministry of Social Affairs and Social Security, the SDCC provides a nationwide service of evaluation of referred children and young people, and subsequent counselling and advice to parents, carers, teachers and therapists. The 2003 SDCC Act (Lög um Greiningar- og ráðgjafarstöð ríkisins nr. 83/2003) states:

> The aim of this Act is to ensure that children with severe developmental disorders which may result in handicaps are provided with diagnosis, counselling and other remedies aimed at ameliorating the consequences of their disorders, and also to ensure the acquisition, maintenance and dissemination of professional knowledge and skills in this field. For this purpose, the state shall operate an institution, the State Diagnostic and Counselling Centre, to serve the whole country. (Article 1)

Day-to-day direction of the SDCC is in the hands of doctors, and it serves individuals with a wide range of impairment, both intellectual and physical (Lög um Greiningar- og ráðgjafarstöð ríkisins nr. 83/2003). Referrals are mostly made by paediatricians, paediatric hospital departments, neo-natal units and by health centres and preschools. Annually, approximately 150 new referrals are accepted (Greiningar- og ráðgjafarstöð ríkisins, e.d.a), with others (including older children who are seen to have relatively mild problems) being placed on a waiting list. Long term follow-up and re-evaluations constitute a significant part of the SDCC's function.

"Each child is evaluated by an interdisciplinary team that works towards a consensus on the child's condition and prognosis. The needs of the child and its family for special services are defined, counselling offered and necessary referrals made" (Greiningar- og ráðgjafarstöð ríkisins, e.d.a). All the parents interviewed for this study were at one time or the other referred to the SDCC or its predecessor, the Kjarvalshús Assessment Center. The SDCC produces the formal label of childrens' difference, a necessary precondition for children and families to access any kind of formal support.

The SDCC has changed and grown over the years. It now employs over 60 mostly highly qualified staff; medical doctors, psychologists, social workers, various therapists, teachers and others. It is divided into three departments; for children labelled autistic, for children with mobility and sensory impairment and for children with intellectual impairment.

The focus has always been from a medical model perspective (Oliver, 1990) on how to assess and habilitate disabled children and, to some extent, young people, but in the last decade it has expanded its work considerably, and emphasizes giving information and support to parents and close family members over longer periods, educating all kinds of professionals and semi-professionals, and informs and advises the government.

REFLECTION

It is difficult to map out the maze of formal support to disabled children and their families over time. Legislation and regulations that impact disabled people and families have changed significantly since 1979, but the general trend of these changes seems twofold. On the one hand new forms of formal support have emerged to fill perceived gaps and accommodate new scientific and professional knowledge and technology relevant to the field of medical model disability issues, and new or extended categories of disability label have increased the numbers of people classified as disabled. On the other hand, general social service legislation has been extended and amended to meet the minimum needs of the population for social and economic security through the SSI.

Chapter 3

METHODS AND DATA SOURCES

This chapter provides an overview of the research project, its data source methodology, its limitations and ethics. In Appendix 2 I include an article on ethical problems in research with people in vulnerable situations. That article is based on this research project, but was first published in Educare 2009, a publication on methodology (Bjarnason, 2009b) and is here reprinted with permission from the editor.

Qualitative inquiry aims to understand the meaning of human action. It involves a type of social inquiry which has its roots in hermeneutics, phenomenology and the tradition of *verstehen*. It encompasses all forms of social research involving data in the form of the words and gestures that underlie meaning making, and a broad base of methods, techniques and theoretical approaches applied to gather and interpret that data (Schwandt, 2001). The present study used qualitative methods largely influenced by the world view aspect of grounded theory technique and hermeneutics (Ferguson and Ferguson, 1995; Glaser and Strauss, 1967). The Fergusons characterise the methodology associated with the interpretive paradigm "as the systematic collection and analysis of the stories people tell about how they interpret reality" (Ferguson and Ferguson, 1995, p. 105).

The primary method of collecting data was interviewing and document analysis. The study began in 2006 involving in all 75 families with disabled children (75 mothers and 51 fathers), born 1974 to 2007[1]. Nine couples asked

---

[1] More parents were interviewed, but I did not use all the interviews, selecting only those that added something new. Interviews with one or both parents of 30 families from a former study on disability and the social construction of adulthood (2004) also informed this research.

to be interviewed together. One parent of a much older adult born in the mid 1960s, and 12 professionals (medical professionals, teachers and administrators) were also interviewed. In addition, I gathered background data from three focus group interviews with staff in disability services in three municipalities. Five couples who chose to abort their foetus because of a diagnosis of difference were also interviewed for the study. Thus the database consists of 140 interviews, and the 3 focus group interviews. The interviews lasted from 45 minutes to 2 hours and 20 minutes. They were all recorded, transcribed and analysed. Three research assistants, students at MA level in psychology, education and anthropology, helped with the work at different times.

The study started with a broad focus on the parents' experiences and interpretations of their lives and the formal (from the health and educational systems and social services) and informal support used over time. The "constant comparative" method was followed where data collection and analysis proceeded together (Bogdan and Biklen, 1992), using within case analysis followed by across case analysis. Several memoranda were written at different stages, and within case and between case triangulations were conducted (Wolcott, 1994, 1995). Additional information was gathered from documents and from the focus group interviews.

Informants were selected by "strategic sampling", that is selected for their ability to provide new insights or to expand or add to gained insights. I included as broad a diversity of parents of children with significant but different disability labels as possible. The families were first contacted through other parents and local professionals. In this study only one mother refused to give an interview. Two families had heard about my study and contacted me to volunteer their stories.

ACCESS

I found it surprisingly easy to gain access. I am known in my society both as a parent of a disabled child (for a time active in the parents' movement) and as an academic. To gain access I called key people in the practical fields of teaching or services for disabled people, explained in general terms what my research was about and enlisted their help in finding suitable research participants. They then contacted individuals who might be willing to talk to me, and after gaining their consent, sent me a list of names and phone numbers. I phoned these people, explained what I was doing and why, and asked for interviews with both parents. My research assistants would then re-contact the parents and set up a date and a time for the interviews. This was complicated because it sometimes involved travelling to places some distance from Reykjavík. Flights, long drives, accommodation and more had to be planned well ahead of time and it was not easy to change interview dates at short notice; parents did not always appreciate this, and quite often the fathers had been called away because of their work, forgot the appointment or thought that it was fine if I only interviewed their wives. Still, I caught up with many of these fathers later, when they granted the interviews willingly. The willingness of parents (particularly the mothers) to participate in this research is gratifying but it also causes me concern. Many of the people I enlisted to help did so because they wanted to contribute their experiences in order to inform and enlighten professionals, politicians and the general public about the fate of their disabled children, and thus combat stigmatization and prejudice. Anonymity was promised to participants, so I have changed names and other facts that might identify the people involved, but it is inevitably hard to disguise research informants in such a small society, particularly when researching the lives of disabled people and their families. This poses challenges related to trust and the protection of the identities of research participants; I have tried my very best to blur or disguise those identities.

My own professional and personal experience over the past three decades, as university teacher and parent of a son with significant impairment, influence my research. This poses methodological and ethical dilemmas. (Bjarnason, 2004, see also Appendix 2, Bjarnason 2009b).

THE SAMPLE

The parents in the study represent the population of Icelandic families as they have evolved from 1974 to 2008. They come from all walks of life. They live in urban areas, in small towns and villages around the country, and on farms. They have different socio-economic backgrounds and education, different sexual orientation, life styles and religious affiliations. Only one family is of mixed Icelandic and immigrant origin because I could not find "new Icelanders" with a significantly disabled child who were willing to be interviewed. Eight families had two disabled children and four had three. Seven families had lost a child through accidents, illness or due to impairment.

Most of the families consisted of "original couples" and their mutual children, but some of these couples had a child, or in one case two children, with a different partner outside or before their current marriages or cohabitations. Twelve couples were in their second and one in their third marriage or cohabitation. Two couples were gay and ten were single parents. Three couples went through a divorce during the time of the research. The number of children per family (children of first and subsequent marriages or cohabitations) ranged from one to nine. One disabled child was in a foster family and one lived with grandparents.

The parents were placed into four groups according to the year of birth of their disabled child or children, and the major milestones occurring in social policy and practices impacting disabled people and their families in that period. I label these groups as *the Explorers, the Pioneers, the Settlers* and *the Citizens of the welfare state.* These groups are not mutually exclusive, as many of the issues reported by one group lingered on despite changes in legislation and services.

In the first group, *the Explorers,* I placed parents of children with disabilities born 1974-1983. 15 families occupy this group; 14 have one child with disability and one family has two. The disability labels are:

Autism	= 2+1
Down's syndrome	= 5
Physical	= 2
Intellectual	= 4
CP	= 1
Multiple	= 1
Other	= 0

Very little formal support was in place for these families.[2]

In the second group, *the Pioneers*, I placed parents of children with disabilities born 1984-1990. 15 families occupy this group; 13 have one child with disability and 2 families have two. The disability labels are:

Autism	= 2
Down's syndrome	= 4
Physical	= 2+1
Intellectual	= 4+1
CP	= 1
Multiple	= 2
Other	= 0

---

[2] In 1973 29.1% of all "inmates" in the institutions were children 15 years and younger, but by 1985 the figure was 8,4% (Margeirsdóttir, 1975).

At the beginning of this period, services (especially services to families with disabled children) outside the two main urban areas were few but in the process of being set up. In the third group, *the Settlers*, I placed parents of children with disabilities born 1991-2000. 25 families occupy this group; 21 have one child with disability, 2 families have two, and 2 families have three children with disability labels. The disability labels are:

Autism	= 7+4
Down's syndrome	= 3
Physical	= 4
Intellectual	= 5+1
CP	= 2
Multiple	= 3
Other	= 1

The biggest changes during this period affecting families with disabled children were to the educational system, and involved a transformation of practice from segregated to integrated and (in some schools) inclusive schooling.

In the fourth group, *the Citizens of the welfare state*, I placed parents of children with disabilities born 2001-2007. 20 families occupy this group; 16 have one child with disability, 2 families have two, and 2 families have three children with disability labels. The disability labels are:

Autism	= 11+4
Down's syndrome	= 4
Physical	= 1
Intellectual	= 3+2
CP	= 1
Multiple	= 0
Other	= 0

The 5 couples interviewed who chose to abort their foetuses after 2001 are linked with this group. This last period under study saw an increase in services around the country; it can be identified as the period of inclusive education (of varying quality) in compulsory schools and preschools.

The Interviews

The interviews took place either in my office or in the families' homes, depending on their preferences and the practicalities. When the interviews were in people's homes, I had the opportunity to meet many of the disabled children or young people along with other children in the families, and observe family interaction and home surroundings. A research assistant was present in 39 interviews in people's homes, and in 14 interviews at the university. Whether or not to include them in the interview situation was partly a budgetary issue. They were of course trained beforehand, and only included with the parents' permission. They would be placed unobtrusively to the side and only brought into the conversation after the interview had been closed. We were frequently served coffee, shown around the house or farm, introduced to other family members, and treated like guests, chatting about this and that. This helped fill in the picture of the family in question. The research assistant wrote notes and comments after the interviews to compare with mine. Twice the assistant had to conduct the interview alone because I knew the informants personally.

The research had been certified by the National Bioethics Committee of Iceland and reported to the National Committee on the Protection and Processing of Personal Data. This is standard procedure under Icelandic law, and the parents were reminded of this at the beginning of the interview, when they co-signed a statement with me to that effect. The National Bioethics Committee requested that parents were given the option of therapeutic counselling by a psychologist paid by the research program if they so wished after the interviews, but no one felt that need or accepted that offer.

Building Rapport

I always began by explaining what I was doing without going into great detail. I talked about what the research was about, explained that I had a list of topics to talk about but not pre-designed questions, promised confidentiality, asked permission to record the interview, and answered any questions they had. I also told them that it was up to them what they chose to tell me, and that we could stop the interview at any time. Further, that if they later regretted what they had said, I would erase the interview and not use it for the research. Then we signed a paper of consent and confidentiality.

I started the interview by asking about the family: "Tell me about the people in your family?" This question provided information on the family structure, number of children, the parents' work, education and previous marital status (if applicable), the children's health, schooling and more. Most respondents found it easy to sketch out a brief description of their families, and the interview could move on. Some parents would also ask similar questions about me and my son, which I was happy to answer. My aim was to balance the interview so that the parents had control over what was being communicated, how and why.

THE INTERVIEW

Next I asked the parent to describe their child (or children) labelled with disability; the child's strengths, personality, charm and needs. Then we moved on chronologically through my interview guide (a list of topics to do with formal and informal support), but parents had ample opportunities to add their own concerns and stories. Many of those stories were filled with emotion (see Appendix 2, Bjarnason, 2009b). Parents were revisiting events and feelings they might not have shared with others before, or not thought about for a long time. The role of the interviewer is not and should not be that of a therapist. There is a fine line between listening to peoples' experiences and becoming their therapist, a line that should not be crossed in the research interview situation. I learnt to keep a box of tissues within reach for the interviewees, but there were also many instances of "smiley voices" and laughter recorded and registered in the transcripts. The parents were talking to me about experiences and emotions they expected me to know and understand as a parent. This not only opened up areas of discussion that a researcher with different experiences might not have entered into, but it may also have prevented me from asking certain questions. The way I listened and interpreted what I heard was framed by my personal knowledge and experience, and I am aware I may have brought some bias into this work. Despite my age and experience, some of these stories touched me to the core. I have come from interviews deep in thought, sometimes smiling, sometimes needing to cry, and even sick to my stomach (see also Bjarnason, 2004, pp. 312 and 315-317 and Appendix 2, Bjarnason, 2009b). Some parents would ask my advice or opinion, which I tried to gather up and respond to when the formal interview was over. I closed the interviews by referring to more practical, immediate and optimistic subjects.

DATA ANALYSIS, TRIANGULATION AND CHECKING, AND THE WRITING UP OF FINDINGS

During the process of reading and rereading both the interviews and the research notes made at various stages of the analysis, the date began to "speak" to us in a new way. Themes emerged within and between data bits. Triangulations were made both within and between cases, as we looked for similar or opposing examples. Sometimes the research participants were contacted for clarification or verification (see for example Bogdan and Biklen, 2003).

During the process of analysis, as in the interviews themselves, I was keenly aware of my own experience as a parent talking to other parents. There is always a danger of the researcher over-identifying with his or her research participants in such situations. To guard against this, my research assistants were involved in the data analysis and coded much of the data independently. We compared codes, notes and themes, discussed interpretations, and triangulated across and within cases. Legal and other written documents were analysed, and the interviews with the professionals and the focus groups were similarly explored. This work is characterized by a constant process of going back and forth between data collection, interpretation and theory development, and consists of a steady formulation of new questions leading to re-interpretation of the data. At that stage I wrote several analytic memoranda (see for example Taylor and Bogdan, 1984; Wolcott, 1995). After data collection was completed I worked on the final analysis of all the material at hand, compiling different pieces of data relating to the themes and patterns I had identified and developing new insights and concepts. As the analytical work proceeded, I also gave twelve papers at various scientific conferences and wrote five articles and book chapters. This helped keep my research moving. The final writing-up process has taken the best part of a year, intermittently, between other work.

Feedback and questions from parents, from my research assistants and from professionals and representatives of parent associations, and from experts and disabled people at public talks and conferences, gave additional insights and information. In qualitative research one is not concerned with discovering the "truth", but rather with the "trustworthiness" of the data and their interpretive accuracy. Thus I am not concerned with discovering an objective "truth", but trying to determine in the data analysis "credibility", "dependability", "consistency", "authenticity" and "transferability". The

Icelandic parents do not speak with one voice. Nor do they speak in unison, but by adding their voices and ideas to the multi-threaded web of our so called "knowledge", we might get closer to understanding what disability in families may involve in time and space. The findings from this study carry a strong "family resemblance" to the findings of other researchers who look at families of disabled children and young people (Ferguson, 2001a; Lundeby and Tøssebro, 2008b; McLaughlin, et al., 2008; Tøssebro and Lundeby, 2002; Ytterhus, Wendelborg, and Lundeby, 2008).

ETHICAL ISSUES

The ethical issues and dilemmas involved in this study are many and taxing. As mentioned above, I have written about some of those in detail in a recent paper *Walking on eggshells* (see Appendix 2, Bjarnason 2009b). These issues touch upon being a parent and interviewing other parents of disabled children; gaining access; the interview situation itself including the building of rapport; the ethical challenges found in the interview situation itself and in the data analysis; disguising the informants; and some concerns in the writing up of sensitive data and its publication. I can now only hope that this work is respectful of the gifts my research participants bestowed upon me, and that their sharing of their experiences and perspectives will have some impact – will help to further an understanding of the problems and pleasures of parenting a child with disabilities during the evolution of social and disability policy and practice in Iceland in the period leading up to the economic collapse of 2008. In the new socio-economic climate, these families are likely to be vulnerable to cuts in education, health and welfare services, which adds to the importance of making their voices heard and responded to. It also adds to my own ethical plight well beyond this study.

Chapter 4

THE OLDER PARENTS: THE EXPLORERS AND THE PIONEERS

The children of the Explorers were born 1974-1983 and those of the Pioneers in 1984-1990. Before support services were in place, having a disabled child was seen as an act of God or fortune, a *private problem* to be dealt with in the families. Support was taken to be an act of kindness or pity. Gradually, however, parents came to expect there to be some kind of formal support available. The perspective shifts slowly from disability in the family being a *private problem* towards it being seen as a *public issue* as well.

THE "TRAGIC CHOICE"

The story of Sigríður and her daughter, Guðrún, in the first vignette of the book, illustrates the tough choice that many parents had to make before formal supports were put in place for disabled children and their families: either to keep the child at home, with little or no help, schooling or other intervention except from the family doctor, or to send him/her to an asylum, if one was available. This was the choice facing the families of disabled children in most of the western world from the middle of the 19th century through to the 1960s (Anonymous, 1951). Despite the difficulties, many parents kept their disabled child at home (Ferguson, 1994, 2008). That was particularly the case in Iceland, where the institutions were slow to appear[1].

---

[1] See chapter 2. In Iceland the first institutions for idiots and the feeble minded opened in the mid 1940s; a few other such smaller institutions were opened up to the early 1980s. An

THE EXPLORERS. FROM NO FORMAL SUPPORT TO A LITTLE BIT

In the early 1960s parents who wanted to keep their disabled children at home but provide them with education, training and support formed an association, *Styrktarfélag vangefinna*, to that end. Much of their efforts were spent on building, organising and running segregated services in the community. This happened in other countries as well, and speaks for parents bonding together in order to solve their *private problems* (Ferguson, 1994; Kirkebæk, 2001, 2007). In 1961, disabled people established *Öryrkjabandalagið*, "The Organisation of Disabled in Iceland". This was, and still is, a powerful umbrella association of persons with physical or sensory impairment, different diagnostic labels, and chronic diseases. It created and operated a "laundry list" of segregated services for disabled people in the coming decades.[2] By the late 1960s and early 1970s a more radical group of parents and a few professionals joined forces, disappointed with the focus of *Styrktarfélag*, and in 1976 formed the advocacy movement *Þroskahjálp*, an umbrella association of parents and professionals, pressing not only for services but also for normalisation, integration and human rights. This group grew in strength and importance and evolved into a powerful pressure group, and was eventually involved (as was *Öryrkjabandalagið*) in shaping the disability legislation and social disability policy. *Þroskahjálp* was instrumental in shifting the focus of government and public opinion from that of disability in the family as a *private problem* to it also becoming *a public issue* based on citizenship and human rights.

Towards the end of the period, community-based services began to be developed, normalisation and integration became the law (Lög um aðstoð við þroskahefta nr. 47/1979), and special schools had opened in Reykjavík.[3] At the

---

institution for orphans and children whose parents could not care for them was established in 1930 along the lines of Anthroposophy and the Rudolf Steiner ideology. That institution became the first institution for disabled children in Iceland. It is still operated, but the approximately 45 inmates are older people with intellectual impairment. In recent years it has been developed into an ecological society (Bjarnason, 1996, 2004; Margeirsdóttir, 2001; Sigurðsson, 1993).

[2] This organisation grew in the 1980s and 1990s (on lottery revenue) and became politically powerful. In 2009 it had 34 different organisations and interest groups under its umbrella, including Styrktarfélag vangefinna. It has evolved into a powerful pressure group for inclusion and human rights, while at the same time expanding its special segregated services.

[3] Education for people who were deaf became available in the late 19th century, and the Deaf School opened in Reykjavík in the early 20th century. Parents with children who were deaf

end of the period the new law on "The Affairs of the Handicapped" (Lög um málefni fatlaðra nr. 41/1983), expanded the group that could benefit under the legislation.

THE PIONEERS. SOME FORMAL SUPPORT BUT NOT VERY MUCH

The extent to which parents could really make use of available services depended on where they lived, whether or not they had relevant information, a car, and whether or not they could take time off from work, their homes and other children.

For people living outside the capital, the journey to Reykjavík with their disabled child, sometimes several times a year, could be cumbersome, expensive and lonely. One father from the *Pioneer* group, for example, reported that he and his wife had driven between 17,000 and 18,000 miles a year for almost 17 years with their two children, one disabled and the other chronically sick, for special services in Reykjavík. Some such trips were subsidised under the law from 1979, but only for one accompanying parent. At the same time the parents had to keep their other children at home and their finances on an even keel. In some instances local municipal authorities helped pay the travel cost – this often depended, however, on the whim of political leaders or bureaucrats of the municipality and the parents' access to those leaders. The extent to which different families accessed and engaged with bridging and linking social capitals impacted on their ability to make use of available services. Better off, better educated, urban parents were more able to make use of the formal support system than were poorer, less educated, rural parents.

From the parents' perspective change seemed very slow. In addition, perceptions of the needs of the families and their disabled children were subject to change. New professional groups were emerging with new skills, for example ergo therapists, more developmental therapists, more physiotherapists and special educators; and parents wanted to make use of their skills for their children's benefit. The standard of living was rising, and most women had

---

were encouraged, and since 1962 (Lög um heyrnleysingjaskóla nr.13/1962) obliged by law to send their children to the Deaf School in Reykjavík at the age of 4 years old. Children from the rural areas frequently became boarders from that age. It has become clear as I write that many deaf children who were boarders suffered sexual and other violence at the school, both from older students and some staff (Forsætisráðuneytið, 2009).

entered the labour force. These parents felt that they too were entitled to similar lifestyles as their neighbours without disabled children.

The efforts of *Þroskahjálp* and others were bearing fruit. There was a gradual shift in public discourse, influenced by the disability lobby and a few academics, towards a *rights* argument, integration, normalisation, and a social model perspective. By 1990, disability in the family was becoming both a *private problem* but also a *public issue*.

THE STRUGGLE

One dominant theme going through all the narratives, including the interviews with the older parents, was the lack of support from extended family and friends. This will be discussed at some length in Chapter 7. Contrary to common belief, it was the exception rather than the rule that the extended family and friends gathered around a family with the disabled child or children. Such informal support was, indeed, often given at the birth of a disabled child, but seemed to wear off with time. People were expected to look after their own, both in the urban and rural areas. Many mothers and some fathers reported losing touch with close family members and old friends. Still, most of the mothers had a sibling, a girl friend, a mother or mother-in-law who provided practical help or listened. But often these people were not close at hand. The families moved (to be closer to special services or to work), leaving their bonding capital behind. And even when the network of family and friends lived nearby, things happened. Misunderstandings and hurt, the child with disabilities not welcomed at family gatherings, complex time-consuming care for some of the disabled children, the needs of the other children, lack of time and money, and the general pace of life; these were all used by the older parents to explain the isolation many found themselves in. Some managed to build new social capital, engaging with other parents of disabled people, and with members of the disability lobby.

The other overarching theme from the data obtained from the older parents was the search for services: first came the struggle for appropriate health services, for assessment, for physiotherapy and speech therapy, for respite, funds and more. The preschools and compulsory education schools also presented the parents with a struggle. Later, these same parents reported struggling to find a suitable group home, a workplace or day support service. Many of the adult disabled children of the older parents stayed at home longer than they and their parents really wanted. When the parents had to give up, for example for health reasons, their disabled sons and daughters were often moved to the first available group home or institution. As sheltered workshops and day centres opened, there were frequently long waiting lists. Time spans for working in some of the new sheltered workshops could be divided between disabled adults, alternating with weeks at home, to make space for others on the waiting list. This caused confusion and interruption to the rhythms, routines and work schedules of all the family members.

DEALING WITH HEALTH CARE

All the parents were asked how and when they got to know that something was different with their child. The themes that emerged were: suspicion and fear, being heard but not taken seriously, waiting and feeling confused and disempowered, negotiating with professionals, the labelling, anomie, the search for relief and resources, and the constant fight.

The parents told of their experiences with the health system and medical experts, the birth, the neonatal unit, or (if the impairment was not immediately recognisable) about the growing fear for the first months or even years of their child's life. These stories were almost without exception very detailed and emotional. A kind word or a smile was still treasured decades later; a clumsy or damaging word or look still hurt.

These parents had the children God, or Fate, gave them. Ultrasound scans were introduced to prenatal services in 1975, but at first only to older pregnant women and women likely to have significant problems in their pregnancy. Two mothers from the *Explorers group* had scans, and eleven in the *Pioneer group*. All were told that their foetuses were fine, though they subsequently gave birth to disabled babies. Some mentioned a possible fault in the equipment, others that the health workers did not interpret the indicators correctly.

With only one exception, the mothers reported their satisfaction with the prenatal services, except where the scan indicated that the foetus might have a difference. Few fathers in these two groups accompanied their wives when they went for scans. In general, reports of the prenatal services included being treated with respect; the midwives, doctors and other health workers being kind and considerate; and that the mothers felt that they were in good professional hands.

Soffía, the mother of Elísabet, born in the late 1980s with CP, described her experience thus:

We had been trying to get pregnant for two years. So I was careful. I went to have prenatal examinations three times. I did everything that I was supposed to do, everything they told me. [The midwife, doctor and staff at the prenatal services] were kind and gentle and took exceptionally good care of me.

THE HUNCH

Some of the parents told how they had suspected that something was not "right" with their unborn child. They talked of "hunches" they could not explain, and strange dreams. The father of Viktor, born in 1974 with physical impairment, told this story:

> I had this weird dream when she was pregnant. I dreamt that we had a baby with a beautiful head...Just perfect. But when I looked closer the baby had a skeleton body. I woke up in terror. I did not mention the dream to anybody, not even the wife. When Viktor was born as he is, I was prepared.

Most of the fathers and the mothers who mentioned such hunches, dreams or unease kept them to themselves until after the birth.

THE BIRTH/DIAGNOSIS

The stories changed when they revolved around the birth itself. In the *Explorers* group, no fathers were present at their child's birth; in the *Pioneers* group a third of them were.

The stories varied. Sometimes the doctor sat down by the bed and took time to explain the baby's difference to one or both parents. These doctors were fondly remembered by the parents. A mother to a disabled child born 1979, said:

> [The doctor] sat on my bed and held my hand and waited until I had stopped shaking. Then he explained. I will always be grateful to that man and I respect him as a doctor.

But a number of the parents had a different story. A father from the *Pioneer* group said:

> The doctor called late at night and told me that [my wife] had given birth to a baby boy who was impaired. He used the word "an idiot". He told me to come to the hospital as soon as possible to be with my wife. She needed my comfort. We could send this child to the institution, and try for another [baby]. I did not know what to say ... I could not believe this. Everything went black ...She was in the hospital [and] there was no one to turn to.

When the baby's difference could be detected almost immediately, or if its condition at birth was such that it had to be rushed into the neonatal unit, the memory of the birth was almost always filled with fear and shock. The mothers spoke about reading the movements and facial expressions of the medical staff when they handled the baby. Typically they found that actions and words did not match. Then these mothers "knew" or suspected the worst. After the infant was rushed away, the excruciating waiting began; mothers were frequently left alone for quite some time, if the father, a friend or relative was not close at hand. They were typically taken to a ward with other women holding their babies, talking, and breastfeeding, or surrounded by well-wishers. A mother whose daughter was born in 1986 said:

> I was in shock. I had seen the baby for a minute, and I knew she was a "mongol". Nobody said anything. My world collapsed, I did not want this child. The fear daunted me. The birth room emptied and went quiet as a grave. Maybe they had forgotten about me. I was totally alone. Then I heard a strange scream. I did not even know that it was me [screaming]. I could not cry...and then somebody came and wheeled me into the ward with mothers and babies.

After what seemed an eternity her husband arrived. The doctor had phoned him and said that his wife had probably given birth to a "mongol". The father did not know what that meant – he could only think of people from Asia, but that didn't make sense. He rushed to the hospital. When he arrived, nobody had yet said anything to his wife about the baby and she had not seen it properly. They wanted to talk but could not because of the other people in the room. Some time later a doctor came in, and explained what he thought had occurred; he said they were doing some tests and would let them know for certain in a few days. Finally, the woman was given a private room, where she stayed until she was discharged. The baby had to stay in the neonatal ward because of some complications. When they eventually could take the baby home, they were still in shock.

Both parents told me, independently of each other, that they had heard little of the doctor's explanations, and what little they heard, they did not understand. There were other people in the room when the doctor came to talk to them, so they did not ask any questions. "He used a lot of Latin words, I was numb, and didn't remember the half of it…", said the father; "He was in such a hurry, looked at his watch and everything. I could not speak. I just wanted him to go", said the mother.

Some parents were told about their baby's impairment without the other parent being present. A number of fathers were told, as in the examples above, by telephone. A few mothers were told about their baby's impairment in front of other patients, guests, junior doctors, medical students and so forth. One mother was told about her son's impairment as she sat in a glass cubicle on full view to all who passed by in the corridor. Clumsiness of this kind resonates through the data, but is more common in the stories told by the older parents.

There were good stories too. Many of the older parents were mostly positive about the professional skills of the doctors and other hospital staff. Repeatedly the parents told me: "we trusted them", "they knew what they were doing", "they have all this education and specialisation". Some parents were also very grateful for the doctor's skills; "He saved the life of our baby," said one mother from the *Explorers* group.

Árni, the father of a child with multiple disabilities born in the mid 1980s, said:

> Our son was born with a life-threatening heart problem and needed an operation that could not be performed in Iceland. Our doctor arranged for us to go to a hospital in London. He helped us fill in the forms [for the SSI], managed to get financial help for both me and my wife, despite the fact that the rules [of SSI] stated clearly that only one parent was entitled to such help. It was touch and go for our son, so the doctor himself accompanied us in the plane to make sure he was safe. We can never thank him enough and it is good to live in a country where people do this for a child like him.

The parents' complaints about the health workers at this stage were mostly about clumsy communication, a superior attitude, lack of time, and lack of tact in choosing where and how to tell them that their child had impairment. Other common complaints were that the medical staff did not listen to the parents, did not answer their questions, or that they told it all too fast, using strange words.

Mistakes did happen on the medical front. Soffia, one of the *Pioneers* who reported that she had enjoyed excellent prenatal care and done everything right, ached with sorrow when asked about the birth of her daughter. The birth took place in a rural hospital. It was overdue and eventually induced. It took her 36 hours to bring Elisabet to the world. She explained:

> Everything went wrong. The monitor that controlled the baby's heartbeat …They did not read it correctly. I was giving birth…there were indications there that something might be amiss. They did not cotton on…, they did not react, there was no doctor at hand as I had been promised…Then when Elisabet came there was "fluid in her lungs" so she could not breathe. They could not find the doctor on call. They tried to call him several times…and then when he finally came, they had to call the paediatrician in town, because the doctor [a junior doctor] was unable to put the tube into her lungs in order to suck up the "fluid". It took at least 20 minutes from when she was born until she was able to breathe. That is why she is as she is.

A few stories are about the mothers being sent with their babies soon after the birth, by ambulance or aeroplane, to the main hospital in Reykjavík. With one family from the *Pioneer* group, the mother and her newborn were sent by plane across Iceland without the father or their extended families being told about this until the next day. The mother remembered it thus: "I was very scared. Everything happened so fast, and they forgot to tell them". This marked the beginning of several months in and out of hospital.

Once at the main hospital, mother or parents were frequently kept waiting, without access to food or a bed, alone, fearful, confused and ignored in the hospital's busy schedule. Still other stories were about giving birth to a "healthy baby" and then finding out gradually that something was amiss.

Tom Booth (1978) argues that the labelling process evolves through four stages from the "arousal of suspicion within the family"; "the prevarication stage", when professionals are dismissive of the babies' problem but appreciative of the parents worries, and uninformative; "the growth of conviction" stage, when negotiations between the parents and the professionals when parents are persuaded to make judgements about their child's fate, framed in the terms of medicine. The forth and final stage is then "the labelling", At that stage, Booth argues that the "degradation" of the child is completed with the diagnosis. At that point in time, parents and doctors arrive at a consensus of the reality of the child's condition which results in establishing the status of impairment and disability. In my earlier work I showed how his analysis also applied to Icelandic mothers (Bjarnason, 2004, pp. 38-39).

In such situations, the mothers told of a growing fear that something was different with their child, and not being heard or taken seriously for months or even years, neither by doctors nor by the people in their personal networks and sometimes not even by their husbands. When the diagnosis was finally established the parents felt a mixture of a shock and relief. This was the case even when the diagnosis implied the hardest news possible for the parents: that the child had a genetic difference that would inevitably lead to its suffering and early death.

Stella and Viðar had two children in the middle and late 1970s with the same genetic difference, leading to early death. When their first-born began to show signs of mobility problems, Stella went from one doctor to the next; they heard her concerns, but did not take her seriously. One advised callipers, another special shoes and physiotherapy, and a third advised a psychologist and medication for Stella's nerves. The misleading diagnosis and conflicting advice she received severely dented her self-esteem and sense of identity; actually aggravated their older child's condition; and led to their having a second child, which they would not have done had they known of the genetic problem. Finally, after a heartbreaking search, they got the correct diagnosis from a young doctor who had specialized abroad in paediatrics and exceptionality. For this they were very grateful. The doctor stayed in contact and supported them for several years. During the period before the final diagnosis, Stella and Viðar had both felt that some professionals, family members and friends blamed them for being inadequate, and for making a big deal out of nothing. The diagnosis changed that.

DEALING WITH ASSESSMENT

In 1974 basic formal support, assessment and some early intervention was provided by the Kjarvalshús centre and a few doctors with expertise in dealing with difference. Kjarvalshús staff also travelled outside Reykjavík to consult with parents, preschools, schools and hospitals; on these trips they tried to locate young disabled children who had not yet been registered anywhere. More children were identified and waiting lists grew, but subsequent local professional help was often non-existent, inefficient or unavailable for other reasons.

The older parents, that is the *Explorers* and the *Pioneers*, were on the whole grateful for the services their child got at Kjarvalshús. "It was a warm and caring place", said one parent. "You stepped into a strange, new, fuzzy but professional world with your baby" said another; and "they were on the whole helpful. The staff really cared", said a third. But feelings of bewilderment and even anger and hurt were also part of these stories. "You came in with your baby and eventually you came out with a retarded baby and a long list of everything that was wrong with it", said one mother. And another parent pointed out that the list of labels highlighted the problems, but suggested very few if any solutions. " It is a relief to know that I was not being hysterical, that something was really wrong, and that it has a name", said the mother of Börkur, a man born in 1981, "but when we returned [home] with all the information, there were no services, no physio, no preschool, nothing…".

The "report meeting" at Kjarvalshús, was the final meeting between the parents and all the experts, when the diagnosis was finally bestowed upon the child and the parents were given a likely prognoses and advice. That meeting could and frequently did turn into an ordeal for the parents. Börkur's father remembered that meeting thus:

> I was so angry, I could not speak… There they all were, and the doctor who knew Börkur the least explained [the diagnosis], everything he could never [do or become]….They were all so educated, so sure and I felt stupid and small. These were my genes. Börkur's problems are my fault. I just took it, said nothing. I even thanked them and then went straight home [an 8-hour drive]. I could not speak, and [my wife] cried quietly all the way home.

For many of the older parents, Kjarvalshús provided the first diagnosis, experience of professional support, and advice on how to help their child on an everyday basis. The medical staff were remembered with mixed feelings. A doctor who for some was seen as being outstanding was described by others as hurtful or rude. Most of the staff, however, were remembered fondly, not least a physiotherapist who in her quiet way gave invaluable guidance to all the parents.

As mentioned above, professionals at Kjarvalshús travelled from time to time to different parts of the country in order to advise and instruct the parents, the local service personnel, teachers and therapists. This was highly appreciated. One mother, who had a child with a particularly complex problem, said:

> The physiotherapist came to our town and worked with her preschool teachers...That helped us tremendously... We did not have to criticise how they worked with our daughter... She showed them what to do and explained it all, and we could somehow relax...

Following the 1986 act on the State Diagnostic and Counselling Centre, the Kjarvalshús service was shut down, and the staff transferred to the new premises of the SDCC. Though based on the work done at Kjarvalshús, the new organisation was given increased responsibilities and funding under the new legislation. From the parents' perspective, some of the cosiness of the Kjarvalshús surroundings disappeared. It became a formal organisation with many more professionals. Still the SDCC was almost the only place parents could approach for help. There parents obtained advice on a broad range of medical issues, practical advice on how to apply for various aids and services, and information on what they and their disabled child were entitled to under the Disability and other legislation. The staff also advised parents on issues related to the child's schooling, and family issues concerning their marriage and their other children. Some parents tried to follow the advice given to them by SDCC experts to the letter, while others found some of the advice too personal, or an intrusion into their family life. "They give us so much homework to do with Stefán, and forget that we are working people with five children", said one mother.

The work at the SDCC was firmly rooted within the medical model of disability (Oliver, 1990) and the director, was and still is a practicing medical doctor. The same person has held the directorship since SDCC opened, combining that work with some hospital duty and his own paediatric practice. Most of the parents interviewed were grateful for the SDCC services, but critical of particular aspects. Some doubted the diagnostic methods and what they felt were sweeping generalisations about their child's competence, based on a few tests done in unfamiliar surroundings.

The father of Pétur, a boy with physical impairment born in 1988, refused to accept the label of "selective mutism" on top of other diagnostic labels given to his son. He explained:

> We knew he was all right in the head, but at first the people at the SDCC did not agree. You see, he was only four years old and very determined. When the staff spoke to him, he simply did not respond. He hated that place. In particular, he hated physiotherapy because each time it hurt him badly, and the [physio]therapist was overambitious, [and] just out of college. [Pétur] could not run away, so he kept silent. He refused to talk to those people. He

was also asked to do things he found silly or uninteresting, so he simply did not comply. At home he both spoke and did many demanding things... and he was beginning to learn to read.

Parents' needs for help for themselves and their child from the SDCC experts varied from one family to the next, and within the same family from one time to the next. This called for flexibility, but some parents found the service grew increasingly more bureaucratic. Parents complained that they did not meet with the same advisers from one visit to the next, they had to repeat their stories, and had to join new waiting lists. Mothers attended more meetings at the SDCC than the fathers did, they also attended the courses on offer by the SDCC more frequently, and read more of the literature provided on exceptionality. When the diagnosis was finally delivered to the parents, some felt (as had some of the parents using the Kjarvalshús services) that their child had been damaged and that everything that was "wrong" with their son or daughter had been highlighted at the expense of his or her strengths, talents and ability. Yet the diagnosis was a relief. It often confirmed what the parents knew already or suspected.

Some of the older parents living on farms or in small villages, in particular parents of children with physical impairment, commented on how the SDCC staff, like the Kjarvalshús staff before them, had helped by calling them or visiting them and their children regularly in their homes, schools, or other local services such as respite, bringing practical help, advice and new ideas. For those parents, this was a prerequisite for keeping their disabled children living at home.

DEALING WITH THE SSI

All the older parents interviewed, as well as most of the younger parents, mentioned having to struggle with bureaucracy, especially with the SSI, to try and obtain grants and technical aids. Amongst the *Pioneers* were Hákon and Lilja, a farmer and his wife, the parents of Arnar, a 19 year old man with a regressive physical disability. An older son had died as a result of the same impairment at the age of fourteen. These parents said they supported each other and did not like to "advertise their and their children's predicament to outsiders". They and their grown children had taken turns to help the two sons at home, including dealing with their personal needs, dressing them and turning them in bed at night. Both boys had osteoporosis, so the parents trusted only themselves or the boy's physiotherapist when Arnar had to be lifted (for example on and off the lavatory). The parents did this for Arnar even when he was at school, stopping by at appropriate times. They also drove him to and from the school, for the same reasons. They saw this care as a natural part of their parenthood. They were positive towards the services their sons had made use of, and expressed gratitude and satisfaction with most of the formal support they had received. They were particularly grateful to the staff at the SDCC, who had provided them with valuable advice, helped negotiate support at the preschool and the schools their sons had attended, helped fill in forms to get technical aids and grants, and had visited their farm regularly, at least twice a year, for years. The parents dreaded the time when Arnar would inevitably be transferred over to adult services; he thrived at school, did well in his studies, and had many friends.

When looking back, only the SSI had proved difficult to deal with. Hákon explained:

> You had to apply to the SSI for everything each time and give them a new medical certificate stating that the boys were still disabled... They grew bigger, and they also deteriorated, which called for new aids of all kinds. Unfortunately our younger son could not use his brother's cast-off technical aids. Their needs were not the same. We also had to apply to the SSI for support grants for each of the boys. At first we had to do that every year, later the rules were changed and we had to apply for the grant every other year, then every fourth year. [In a bitter voice] We got tired of this and I told the staff at the SSI once : "They are still disabled. That has not changed. I have no greater wish in my life than that my children would no longer be disabled next year". This was plain stupid. ...Our sons had to get services in the nearest town (45 miles there and back from the farm) and they [SSI] had to pay the equivalent of their bus fares. They did so in the first year, but the year after they [SSI] were expected to cut costs, so they offered to pay the equivalent of only one return fare for both of them on the grounds that the boys were using the same car. I found this ridiculous expecting them to sit, two in the same seat, without anyone to accompany them. They could not travel by bus, because of the state of their bodies. Of course we drove them but the bus money had helped with the petrol [laughter]... later [in the mid 1990s] they were both in wheelchairs and got motorized chairs. We finally got a grant to help buy a car for them, and a loan to fix it up with a lift, and some petrol money.,. It was fine, we are grateful, but it took time, paperwork...and it always felt as if we were begging...

Independence, self-sufficiency, and taking care of your own are ingrained values in the Icelandic culture. Asking for formal support because of a private problem was hard for many parents. It had negative connotations in the public's mind, being associated with destitution and the old poor law legislation in Iceland (Gunnlaugsson, 1982, 1997). Thus, the shame of having to ask for and accept community help lingered on for much of the 20th century in people's minds. The parents, especially the *Explorers* but also several of the *Pioneers,* found it hard to break with that perspective even after being entitled to formal support by the legislator. This was especially difficult and humiliating if the services they needed were only available in the main urban areas. A mother of a boy with hearing and intellectual impairment said that the director of their local authority had pointed out that her son had cost the community too much money, and advised her to move her family to Reykjavík. She said with tears in her eyes:

> How dared he? This has been my husband's family home for generations. They know us. They know that we always pay our due, taxes and such. This is our home and our livelihood is here…We do not owe anybody anything and the SSI foots most of the bill…

As mentioned before, technical aids and grants were funded by the taxpayer and allocated through the SSI. Parents often felt mortified and angry if they asked the SSI for specific aids for their child but were turned down because of the way the bureaucratic rules were framed. That could happen when their child did not precisely fit the definition of the group of disabled children entitled to a particular technical aid or financial support. The diagnosis, for example, might not be considered severe enough to justify the equipment; or the SSI experts might consider the child incapable of operating the equipment (e.g. an electric wheelchair), whereas the parents were of a different opinion. The SSI experts and the parents were frequently at loggerheads over whether or not the family qualified for particular grants.

DEALING WITH EDUCATION

Sigríður, portrayed in the first vignette of the book had no possibility of sending her daughter to school. The oldest parents, *the Explorers*, had, like Sigríður, little or no access to schooling for their disabled children; typically, for them the institution was the only solution. Gradually in the late 1970s and early 1980s, however, educational opportunities emerged in special schools, special classes, and two special preschool units in the two main urban areas. All the parents were concerned about their children's education. In both groups, there were parents like Sigríður, who accepted what their children were offered, but many more who devoted considerable time and energy to lobby for what they saw as appropriate education for their disabled child.

At first this involved getting access to a special school or preschool. Later other parents' concerns revolved more about what actually happened in school both socially and pedagogically. Some of the older parents argued for more specialised educational services. Others (a growing number of parents) wanted their disabled children served by the local schools and preschools (Bjarnason, 2002). The new "integration" movement was impacting these parents. Outside the main urban areas, parents advocated "integrated schooling", based on their need to continue living and working in their home areas. These perspectives are well documented in the data.

Times were changing. Despite much resistance from many headmasters and regular teachers, gradually the barriers were lowered and more schools opened their doors to disabled students. Indriði and Valborg, the parents of a girl with disabilities born in 1984, discovered that there was no place for her in any of the local preschools. They had to accept the situation or move all their family to the capital. They worried about getting their daughter into their local compulsory education school and started to work on that. Three years later, after several letters, phone calls, meetings with the headmaster, the local educational school board, and finally a meeting with the Minister of Education, the local school was forced to take her in. Her father said: "The staff at school looked after her and made her work on her books in the staff-room 8-12 hours a week. She was never with the other children." She was in her local school but unable to become an active learning participant of that school.

Snorri and His Family: Through the Steeplechase

The story of Snorri, born in the late 1980s, illustrates the relentless campaigning for education of their disabled children that many parents of the time engaged in, and highlights the drastic changes in educational opportunities for disabled learners in the late 1980s and 1990s.

Snorri was born with Down's syndrome. His parents are middle class, educated people, with two older children. When Snorri was born, the doctor said to his parents: "Only very few *such children* learn to read, and if very lucky, he might be able to become a newspaper boy as an adult". His mother managed to get Snorri into a regular preschool with the support of a non-professional "good woman". That worked well. Snorri was included and found friends. The professionals at the SDCC advised that he should be enrolled in the special school for the most severely impaired students (children with IQ below 50) on the grounds that it would be better for him to be one of the most able students in that school, than amongst the weakest in the other special school (for students with IQ 50-75). But his parents had other plans. They wanted him to attend his local general school along with his preschool friends.

They had several meetings with the head of that school, and asked if Snorri could be admitted for a year to see if it worked out. The headmaster was firmly opposed to this idea. He told the parents that "Snorri would never get any friends at the school" and asked them how they would deal with Snorri "if he covered his classmates' books in saliva and snot". After a few meetings with this headmaster and staff from the local educational authorities, they gave up and turned to the headmaster of the "higher level" special school. "He received us well and had obviously been well briefed. He knew all about us in advance", said the mother. Snorri attended that school for the next 10 years. Despite it being a special school with individualised teaching, the parents felt that Snorri was not appropriately challenged in his learning. His mother said:

> His teacher did not believe in him, not that he could learn. We never believed that, we knew ... I tried to get [the teacher] to use Snorri's interest in soccer to teach him other things. Snorri knew all the players, their names, numbers and the colours of his favourite club. But the teacher did not listen. ..I never liked that teacher…We worked with Snorri at home. Somehow he never had any homework.

Snorri became very depressed at school and when he was approaching his 12th year refused to attend. He still could not read, and felt that he was left out of the lessons and conversations at school. His parents complained yet again and suggested a new evaluation and a new IEP plan. This time they were heard. The IEP was altered, and a new teacher, interested in Snorri, took him on. Snorri's situation changed dramatically. By his 13th birthday he could read, and between the ages of 13 and 16 he blossomed at school. He now had homework; at first his father helped him with this, but later Snorri did it by himself, showing it to his parents when it was all done. When he graduated, he was given a statement, but no grades. He was lucky, because the legislation opening up special classes for disabled learners in upper-secondary schools had recently been passed. He was accepted into the special class by one such school. He did four years at upper-secondary school. Yet again his parents had to struggle with the school authorities to find out what went on in school and what he was being taught. They were eventually informed and consulted, and came to trust the school. In those years Snorri took up a new sport, ice-skating, and was invited to participate in the Special Olympics in Tokyo 2004. He matured and learnt how to keep track of his time and commitments. His parents had to learn to step aside and give him more space to do his own thing. In 2007 Snorri was one of 22 students with intellectual disability who were selected for university education. An experimental program was set up at the Iceland University of Education for disabled students interested in working in, or in connection with, education. These students studied alongside developmental therapy students, and did their practicum in schools, preschools and other places serving both able-bodied and disabled children and young people. Snorri and his fellow students graduated with a valid diploma and marketable skills. He got a job in his field, and his boss describes him as able, conscientious and a highly reliable employee. He himself and his parents are proud as punch. His mother said, thinking back to his birth:

> Times have changed. Newspapers are no longer sold on the streets of Reykjavík, and my Snorri has proved all the experts wrong. I knew he had it in him. He is such a wonderful and extraordinary guy.

Snorri's parents are part of the Pioneer group. His mother has campaigned relentlessly for changes both at the policy level and in practice, both in the educational and in other formal support systems. She has been active in the parents' movement, and bonded with many other parents of disabled children. They also have a small but close-knit family and several friends who have provided encouragement and help. They are some of those strong parents who have been able to engage to the full with their social capital, and moved the boundaries of what is seen to be possible.

DEALING WITH OTHER SERVICES

The *Pioneers* certainly benefited from the 1983 law and the *Explorers'* advocacy, yet they found that even when formal supports were in place, the value of that support to the disabled child and the family was not always what they hoped for. One example is the provision of "support families" for children with disabilities, as prescribed in the Disability legislation. Support families were paid to take a disabled child into their own families for one or two weekends a month. But support families were hard to find, unless they were relatives or friends, partly because the payment for this service was so small.

A respite service for children under the age of 12 developed early in Reykjavík, then gradually in other towns. The Reykjavík service was considered by the parents who used it to be of high quality and relatively flexible, although there were still waiting lists and formal rules to deal with. Parents learnt to trust it, and many made regular use of it, but such respite services became something of a mixed blessing: as they became available in most parts of the country in the 1980s and 1990s, in some service areas children and young people with significant impairment got used to spending much of their time in such places. Where other services were less available, especially in some rural areas, a few parents appeared to give up the struggle, using the local respite services for their disabled children for several days most weeks. Some such children can be described as being moved from place to place, from home to respite to a support family and back home again, living in a suitcase for much of their late childhood and adolescence.

Summer camps for disabled children and young people, mostly initiated by parents, began to emerge, as did sheltered workshops, group homes and day centres. All these places were small, segregated institutions, developed under the disability legislation from 1979 and 1983. This growth in segregated services was an unintended by-product of the disability legislation and the parents' advocacy.

PARENT ADVOCATES

Many of the oldest parents pushed for changes for their own disabled child, thus affecting both policy and practice. Some spoke of meetings with government ministers, politicians at national and local levels, headmasters, teachers and many other professionals. One father built ramps at every school his son attended. He also made his farm completely accessible, rebuilt their home for the same purpose, and created and ran the local parents' association (a regional chapter of *Þroskahjálp*). Many of these parents generalised from their and their children's experiences and became advocates for all disabled children and their families, using much of their free time doing voluntary work for the parents' movement. In the early 1980s the parent movement bought a house where parents of disabled children could stay at minimum cost while doing their errands in Reykjavík. A number of strong parents amongst the *Explorers* and the *Pioneers* became known for their extensive and effective voluntary work, both locally and at the national level. They set up branches of the parent movement in their communities, or worked at the central office of *Þroskahjálp*. They took part in committee work at both national and municipal government levels, helping to shape legislation affecting disabled people and the national disability policy. They built and organised accessible summerhouses for families with disabled people, set up summer camps and festivities, held meetings with politicians and the public, advocating human rights, education, integration and extra support for disabled people and their families. They held conferences where some of the best known international scholars in the field of disability, education, supported living, supported work and human rights were invited to share their knowledge. They connected with similar advocacy organisations abroad, particularly in the other Nordic countries. These parents, able to generalise from their and their children's experiences, were relentless in their efforts to try and improve the lot of all disabled people and their families. They did not hesitate to pull that particular wagon, even at significant personal cost. All families with disabled children, and disabled adults benefited from these efforts. Disability in the family was gaining recognition as a *public issue*.

Chapter 5

THE YOUNGER PARENTS: THE SETTLERS AND THE CITIZENS OF THE WELFARE STATE

The Settlers had their disabled children in 1991-2000 and the Citizens in 2001-2007. Having a child with disabilities during the period of the Settlers gradually came to be seen as a *public issue* as well as a *private problem*. Parents came to expect that there was some formal support available and that their disabled child and the family had *rights,* as citizens of the state, to extra health services and assessment, schooling, respite, technical aids, grants and subsidies, and more. Formal supports were increasingly seen as a *right* inscribed in law, and services were more and more expected to be adequate, individualised, flexible and of high quality. This is most clearly reflected in the perspectives of the youngest parents, the Citizens.

Different kinds of service were in place, largely free of charge to individual families, but accessibility to these varied according to where a particular family lived and the child's disability label(s). Disability became an issue of various formal organisations at state and municipal levels, and of private organisations. Giving birth to a disabled child also became an issue of choice in some cases, as we moved into the late 20th and early 21st century.

THE TRAGIC CHOICE REVISITED?

Since the mid 1980s normalization, integration and, later, inclusion have been in vogue in both policy and practice (Bjarnason, 1996; Kirkebæk, 2001; United Nations, 1994, 2006) As a result, large institutions and "children's group homes" (small institutions for children with intellectual and often other impairment) were on the way out. For example, Sólborg, an institution for children and adults with intellectual impairments, opened in 1969-70, was closed down in 1984, with the inmates being relocated in group homes. Times changed and "Styrktarfélagið", the parent movement of the 1950s that had argued for and worked hard at establishing segregated services (institutions, group homes, day centres for children and for adults, sheltered workshops, rehabilitation centres and other such segregated services) remained in practice, but their ideology lost some of its appeal and was gradually updated.

In the wake of changing ideology, disability policy-makers focused on integrative and later inclusive practices, as well as setting up more and more small segregated services. In the 1980s and 1990s, some parents began to press the government to establish "small homes" for children with autism and children with multiple disabilities. The first such "homes" opened in the mid 1980s for 5-8 children. There were few of them – two in Reykjavík and a third in Akureyri. They were intended for disabled children whose parents were either dead or unable, despite the availability of home help and respite services, to care for their children in their homes. A few parents from amongst the *Settlers* and the *Citizens* joined forces and argued for more such children's homes. A father of a child with autism born in the mid 1990s said:

> He should be long gone from our home. I love him, but he is too difficult to handle and the wife cannot cope. It is damaging her health. I cannot wait to get my life back. It is better for him and for us if he could be taken care of by professionals, in a suitable children's home. But there is no available space. We have no option…

This father applied for such a placement when his child was only five years old, and lobbied the local authorities regularly for the establishment of a children's home within his municipality. His wife, somewhat subdued, did not agree with her husband. She said:

> My son can be very difficult and embarrassing. He does not like wearing clothes and has been known to run around naked in the neighbours' homes and gardens, but he is my child. I want him to stay at home until he is older, like other kids…Why can't his father understand…?

Sara, a mother of two boys and a ten-year-old girl with profound impairment, had for years battled to have her daughter institutionalized. She organized a small group of similarly situated parents and eventually achieved her goal. When I met her first, before her daughter was institutionalized, she said:

> She needs [the hired staff and health workers'] help when she is not in the respite service. We have no privacy. It is hard, my kitchen is sometimes like a bus stop with strangers coming and going…But [my husband] does not want her to move out…I do not understand why. We could always visit her when we wanted to. We all love her, especially her father.

The second time I met Sara, she was beaming, was tanned and looked years younger than on my first visit. She explained that her disabled daughter had been moved to a new, small children's home. She was happy that she had won her fight and been able to go with the rest of her family on a holiday to Spain for the first time in years. Her husband was torn between his wife's satisfaction and his own unease and sadness. He had, he told me, without Sara's knowledge, even tried to get the authorities to buy a house next door for the "children's home", but without success. He said: "I miss her no end and go and see if she is OK every day. It is different for me. The wife took care of the others while I took care of our daughter…"

A young mother of the *Citizen* generation published an article titled: *Are our children forgotten in the economic boom?* in her local paper and followed it up in her blog.

She wrote:

> Respite services in… municipality are in a desperate state. Two individuals with multiple disabilities live there day and night because we lack a group home….I can no longer work because of my child's illness. Despite many attempts and an emergency situation at home, my son's services have been cut due to lack of space, money and staff. Is this the best we can do for them? (Jarlsdóttir, 2008 my translation).

In an interview with a newspaper she gives her son's diagnosis as autism, mental retardation, ADHD and more. She says: "I am completely exhausted. .. All doors are closed to us…[the boy is described as in need of 24/7 care]. It would be best for us and for the boy if he could get into a special home where developmental therapists and other professionals could work with (Baldursdóttir, 2008) him…" In response to this plea, the director of her local disability service office is quoted as saying "There are around 20 disabled children on our waiting list [for a children's home]. We urge parents to apply for placement for their disabled children if they have not done so

(Baldursdóttir, 2008) already". Here the disability is squarely placed as a public (medical) issue even though living with the child is still seen as a private problem, too hard to deal with in the very busy modern family.

THE SETTLERS. FORMAL SUPPORT IN PLACE?

At the beginning of this period the current disability legislation from 1992 became law (see Chapter 2 and Appendix 1). The stated purpose of the 1992 Disability Act is "to secure all disabled people equity and a comparable quality of life to that of other citizens and create the conditions that enable them to lead a normal life" (Lög um málefni fatlaðra nr. 59/1992, clause 1). Most basic supports and services were supposedly in place both at the municipal and the state levels. This law is still in effect in 2010. As mentioned before in Chapter 2, when other public services such as compulsory schools were devolved to the municipal authorities in 1996, the disability services were, with the exception of the experimental municipalities, still under the administration of the state. The regular schools continued with integration and even inclusion of labelled children in special classes and, increasingly, in regular classes. Students with disability labels became a common sight in almost every class and school (Marinósson, 2007). This was debated by teachers and principals, as many felt that schools had too little available support or skill to educate labelled students, particularly students seen to have significant impairment or behaviour problems. The schools' response was to attempt to improve support, special education options, school psychology services and diagnostic services. The SDCC improved and expanded its services, but there were still long waiting lists. New labels such as ADHD became common, and more children were diagnosed on the autism spectrum.

THE CITIZENS OF THE WELFARE STATE. GREAT EXPECTATIONS

The *rights* discourse gained impact, and inclusion became the new buzzword in the 1990s and even more so in the new millennium. Disability was more and more seen as a public issue, and families with disabled children expected their rights and those of their children to additional quality services to be upheld. The disappointment when that did not work as smoothly as the parents expected can be clearly seen in the second vignette of this book, the story of Mary and Peter.

A DIFFERENT STRUGGLE

Securing Services in the Boom Years

Like many of the parents in the two older groups, many of the younger parents felt that they had to rely on each other as a couple, if the marriage or cohabitation remained intact. Little or no practical support came from family and friends to most of these parents. After a slight economic setback in Iceland in the 1990s and at the beginning of the decade, full employment characterised the economy and there was an influx of foreign workers to man the wheels of the boom.[1] The economy was heating up, affecting urban and rural areas differently, rural areas being less affected than urban areas. Society was changing at breakneck speed, particularly in the urban areas, and with it people's hopes, dreams and expectations.

All this affected families with disabled children. Formal resources were largely in place, at least in the urban areas and in some of the experimental municipalities, but parents who did not get adequate professional advice on how to access them found it increasingly difficult to figure out the maze of bureaucracy, especially the SSI. Furthermore, many parents' expectations for individualised and flexible special services for their children increased, while

---

[1] After a temporary recession in the early 1990s, economic growth was strong, about 4% per year on average from 1994, and Iceland became one of the wealthiest countries in the world according to OECD statistics. Iceland became a member of the European Economic Area in 1994. The economic system was changing rapidly. The national banks were privatised in the middle of the 1990s and the system was heating up rapidly (Hagstofa Íslands, e.d.b).

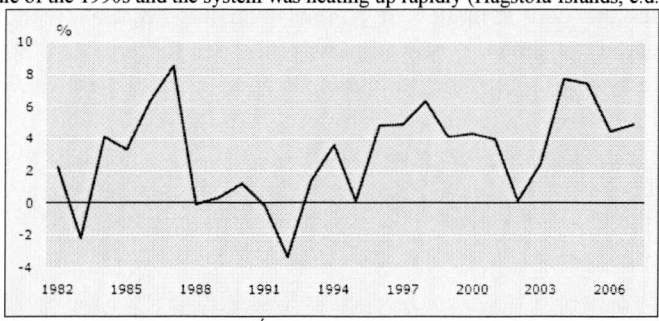

Economic growth 1982-2007 (Hagstofa Íslands, e.d.b).

their belief in and approach to the professionals appeared less submissive than that of the older parents (Bjarnason, 2009a). Parents' choices increased, but the range of services to choose from depended on where in the country the families lived. Parents from the countryside still had to obtain services for their children in Reykjavík, sometimes several times a year.

DEALING WITH HEALTH CARE

When parents of the *Settlers* and *Citizens* groups were asked how they got to know that something was different with their child, the same themes emerged as before but in a slightly different context. They indicated suspicion and fear, being heard but not taken seriously, waiting and feeling confused and disempowered, negotiating with professionals, the labelling process, anomie, and the search for relief and resources. But for these parents, their expectations that services would be available, and that a disabled child in the family was not just their private problem, became clear.

Parents of children whose impairment was clear and easily recognised from birth, like Down's syndrome, found it for the most part reasonably straightforward to get adequate support from the health services. This holds especially true for those parents who lived in some of the larger experimental municipalities, where professional services, good schooling and other resources were in place. But if the impairment was less clear or was complex, many of these parents were in for struggle and disappointment. The story of Mary and Peter in the second vignette in this book, illustrates how educated and highly busy parents had to struggle to get what they thought of as reasonable services for their daughter, how they managed to jump various queues through their contacts, and how disappointed they were with the services they and their child were provided with. That story illustrates well aspects of "the new struggle" of parents who had children with complex labels, and did not simply accept what was provided for them and the child by the service systems. From the professionals point of view these were difficult parents.

Prenatal Services

All but three of the mothers in the younger parent groups had ultrasound scans, most of them twice. Some of these parents had to face the choice of whether or not to let their impaired child be born. The *Settlers* and the *Citizens* could thus well be called the *choice generation* (Bjarnason, 2009a).

As before, most of the mothers expressed satisfaction with the prenatal services. What was changing was that prospective fathers were frequently included throughout the process. Many fathers expressed their satisfaction with that and felt they were participating in the pregnancy in a unique way. One father said:

> When we were pregnant we had the ultrasound three times, and all seemed in order. It was a wonderful experience, and the midwives and other people at the clinic were great ...We were lucky, we had the same midwife all the time.

Most of the fathers in the Settlers group and almost all of the fathers in the Citizens group attended the birth of their child, and most made use of paternity leave when it became available to men. One father described the experience of the birth of his child thus:

> I was exhausted and stressed out. It was a difficult birth and it was hard to see her suffer ... I could not do much, but I tried ... and we are both glad I was there. When it was all over I cried with happiness...

Is something Wrong with Us?

Gunnhildur was born in the mid 1990s. She has a regressive disorder, a genetic problem that in all likelihood will shorten her life. Her intelligence is normal but she has gradually lost the use of her limbs. Her parents, Arnór and Karitas (a craftsman and an artist), lived with their three children in a small rural town just over an hour's drive from Reykjavík. When Gunnhildur started to walk her parents began to suspect that something was amiss. She walked differently from their other children at that age. They took her to the family doctor several times in one year. Each time he said Gunnhildur was fine, but sent her on to different specialist. Each time they returned home with the assurance that there was nothing wrong. The parents were beginning to believe that there was something wrong with them rather than with their child. They did not talk about this to outsiders; they buried their fear. On the one hand they desperately wanted to believe the doctors, but on the other hand they realised, without anything being said, that friends and neighbours were beginning to suspect that something was different. In the summer when Gunnhildur was in her fourth year, a young locum doctor came to town. She noticed Gunnhildur's movements and referred her immediately to a child neurologist in Reykjavík. He took some tests, and told them "this is definitely not muscular dystrophy". They thought this sounded optimistic, but the doctor then went on holiday, so that they had to wait for the diagnosis. When it finally came "it hit like a sledgehammer". They were directed to see a social worker but instead went directly home. Karitas said:

> [The neurologist] gave us some statistics, told us how many individuals in Iceland had the same problem …but you do not know what that means. The deterioration takes time. We learnt about a 17-year-old boy in Reykjavík with this diagnosis. He used callipers. We were told that he had competed in some sport. So I convinced myself that this might not be so terrible after all. A little later an occupational therapist came from the SDCC to look at our house. She pointed out that there was little space for a wheelchair in our home. I thought: What are they talking about? The doctor told us about a 17-year-old with callipers and they are talking about a wheelchair…

These parents got involved with other parents of children with the same diagnosis, learnt from them and set out to help and support new parents. This gave rise to a tiny parent advocacy group fighting the consequences of this particular genetic difference. As they learnt more, and as Gunnhildur's needs changed, they set out to get every formal support available, including technical aid, to help their daughter and keep her at home. Arnór explained:

> It is like searching for a needle in a haystack. It is much better to share the knowledge with other families, instead of having all of us searching for the same thing. You see, nothing comes to you without effort. What you expect will happen does not in fact come your way. You have got to search for yourself, and of course some parents give up. Many people have not got enough strength. But we have got to go on…

SOMETHING IS DIFFERENT – THE BIRTH OR DIAGNOSIS

Both prenatal and postnatal services changed in 1991-2007. In the early 1990s not every pregnant woman had access to the prenatal ultrasound diagnosis. Gunnar, the father of Stefán, born 1992 with Down's syndrome, said:

> My wife Dagný was worried during her pregnancy. She has a sister who is disabled due to an illness. She asked for an ultrasound but was denied it. The doctor told her she was not old enough for that. But had she had the ultrasound, I am not sure what we would have decided...

Gunnar was present at the birth. When Stefán was born, both parents realised immediately that he had a difference. "It came out of the blue", said his father. They knew nothing about Down's syndrome. They asked the doctor if Stefán would be able to walk, talk or need a wheelchair for the rest of his life. Gunnar said:

> ... The doctor was wonderful. He explained that we would have to wait and see... He was kind, polite and informative ...[Irony in his voice] Later one of the "big professors" came. I will never forget that. He said something very negative about people with Down's syndrome. Then he asked me if I understood that the boy was a "mongol". He behaved like a fool...then luckily his bleeper went off, and he left us saying, "OK, I am done here", and he walked out.

Lovisa, born in the mid 1990s, had multiple impairments and suffered from epilepsy from birth. Her mother, Sylvia, is Icelandic but Tomas, her father comes from Eastern Europe. The mother was informed about the medical problems and possible solutions by the hospital staff. Their professional focus was on the baby. Medical technology apparently saved Lovisa's life, for which the parents were deeply grateful. Still, the care for the mother, who stayed two weeks in the hospital, was impersonal. Sylvia said:

> We were in and out of the hospital for almost a year. It was not until ten months after the birth that somebody [from the services] asked me how I was doing. I remember it well, a social worker with the SDCC asked me that question.

Tomas came to visit each day but nobody spoke to him, no one spoke his language. Sylvia's extended family was dealing with her father's terminal illness and death and had little to offer in support. Sylvia's best friend lived abroad and she lost contact with girlfriends, some for good, others for a while. The neurologist working with the child appeared distant and arrogant at first. Sylvia found him difficult to get hold of and the parents felt desperately helpless and alone. They supported each other. Yet they had to deal with a communication problem because neither spoke the other's language with much sophistication. Still they were young and in love, and they lived in the hope that their child's problems could somehow be solved. The doctor picked an unfortunate place to tell Sylvia that her baby "would always have serious epilepsy and multiple impairment". This happened when Sylvia brought two-month-old Lovisa to the hospital for yet another consultation. The doctor delivered his diagnosis and prognosis in a room next to the staff room. The door was ajar, and they could have been overheard by laughing staff on their coffee break. The doctor left immediately, explaining that he had to rush off to a meeting. Despite this, Sylvia and Tomas learnt to trust that doctor and appreciate his help, though they could never quite forget his clumsiness.

Too many such stories appear throughout the data – frequently in the *Settlers* narratives, but somewhat less so in the data from *the Citizens* . Medical technology improved steadily through this period but the hospital staff's bedside manner apparently less so. When something was different with the child, staff mostly focused attention on the child, often forgetting its parents. This also occurred when the child's impairment was diagnosed long after the birth, and the parents had taken their disabled child to see yet another doctor or specialist.

Still, the evidence also includes many stories of considerate hospital staff or medical workers, who did all they could to support the parents in difficult situations. These stories are very precious to the parents. They are all about "the good professional", someone who listened, heard what the parents were saying, treated the parents as equals, spoke a language they understood, was flexible and prepared to go the extra mile to help them, and most of all a person who cared (Bjarnason, 2009a).

THE CHOICE GENERATION

The younger parents had their disabled children in a new era of knowledge, technology and new prenatal services available to all. When the ultrasound scan and subsequent tests showed significant foetal difference, the potential parent(s) faced the difficult choice of whether or not to terminate the pregnancy. A different dilemma was faced by those couples who had done everything that the medical experts had advised, but still had a child with impairment (Bjarnason, 2009a). As mentioned above, the *Citizens* and many in the *Settlers* made use of the prenatal ultrasound technology at least twice during the pregnancy. Most reported having been told that there were no problems, but others had a different tale to tell.

Katrín and Viktor lived in the urban area. They had their first child soon after their marriage in 1999. Life was good and in 2002 they expected their second child. When Katrín was in her 19th week of pregnancy, the couple went for her ultrasound scan. She said:

> There was something in the air, but nothing was said directly. When we came out of the ultrasound, we were made to wait in the corridor. Other parents came out on cloud nine, beaming with joy. We were different. The waiting was hard and seemed to take forever.

It emerged that the foetus seemed to be missing a section of intestine, and it was suspected that there might be some more problems. These things were hinted at but not stated directly. The couple had more tests done. They came out fine, but the doctor suspected Down's syndrome and urged them to have further tests done by invasive diagnostic procedure[2]. They agreed.

Viktor said:

> We did it without thinking. It seemed logical... We were told that we could have an abortion up to the 22nd week of pregnancy. That surprised both of us. I thought that it was absurd. It is murder. If you look at a foetus at that stage it has a human form, it is a baby. [The doctor] told us that on average 5- 8 "mongols" were diagnosed at the foetal stage each year in Iceland, and last year all the women had an abortion. We did not think they were putting us under pressure, they just told us this clearly and clinically as cold facts. I invited the answer by asking how many of these pregnancies had been terminated.

They were provided with information by the hospital staff. This included that the intellectual impairment due to Down's syndrome could be more or less

---

[2] In many countries, an invasive diagnostic procedure is generally offered when the estimated risk is in the range of 1:300 or higher, corresponding to the chances of giving birth to a child with Down's syndrome associated with maternal age of 35-36 years. The invasive procedures, chorionic villus biopsy or amniocentesis, carry a risk of foetal loss in the range of 1:100. If a chromosomal aberration is confirmed by invasive testing, the therapeutic options are to terminate the pregnancy or to prepare for the arrival of the child (Getz and Kirkengen, 2003, p. 2047).

serious, that some such children were quite active, that some had a heart defect, a diminished possibility of schooling, dependent adulthood, and so on. Shortly before Christmas, the test results came. They were told that the foetus did not have Down's syndrome, but that there were problems with its intestines.

They were over the moon with joy and felt that they had got the best Christmas present ever. The baby was taken directly to the neonatal unit after the birth. The parents were prepared for that. But the next day the doctors and the midwife appeared. Katrín said:

> We were told, I cannot remember it exactly, that she was blind or that she had very severe disability. [The doctor] said that this baby was "seriously underdeveloped". I will always remember those words. He did not explain this much further, no one did...

While at the hospital a clergyman, a family member, came twice to see them and provided much-appreciated support, as did Katrín's sister and some close friends. A social worker visited briefly. Katrín's mother came, but her visit was problematic: her second husband had a brother with intellectual impairment and she somehow brought the difficulties of that experience to her daughter's bedside.

The couple reacted differently to this experience. She broke down and cried, he did not. She spent a lot of time in the neonatal unit, he would not, saying that while he sat next to his baby's cot, where she fought for her life, he dared not bond with her; he was too scared of losing her. The baby had her first operation when she was less than two days old, she stopped breathing a few times, and slept very badly for months to come. According to Viktor, while still in the hospital, a doctor asked them whether or not to continue the baby's treatment.

Viktor said:

> The doctor asked: "Do you want her to live or die?" How could he ask us this? We felt there was such a lot of strength in our baby...despite everything. I think they only saw her disability, her *tremendous disability* as they put it...We always saw a lot more... we saw our daughter. When we left the hospital, they told us she would only survive a few months... [laughter] I had almost forgotten that, you tend to forget difficult things...We were sent home with medicine. The doctor said we were playing at being Pollyanna. One could always try, but that the medication would probably not help...

When they finally returned home with their baby, ten weeks after her birth, family members helped. They were glad to be home, and decided to enjoy whatever time they would get with their daughter. It has been tough going, but she is still alive, living with her parents, using respite services and attending a special school. Her health is precarious, but with the combination of support from family, friends and the service system, she is doing well.

These parents did not have to choose whether or not to have their child. Their "Christmas Present" took care of that. Despite the medical and technological advances, they got the child that was given to them. Once that child was born they knew that as long as their daughter lived there were people in their informal network to support them, and resources out there to help. Their ability to engage with social capital proved invaluable. Other parents had to face making a dreadful choice.

TO HAVE THE BABY OR NOT?

I have written elsewhere about the dilemma of the parents of Vera (Bjarnason, 2009a). Here I revisit their story, because they provide a good example of parents caught in the dilemma whether to abort or have a disabled child.

Ólafur and Sólveig are part of the *Settlers* group. Their daughter, Vera, was born with a genetic difference in the late 1990s. Sólveig experienced some bleeding in her 16th week, had her first prenatal screening, and the couple was assured that everything was fine. In the 19th week they went again for screening afterwards, they were sent out of the room and told to wait for the doctor, and that another ultrasound scan had to be done. Then the obstetrician came and they were told that something was not right with their unborn baby's brain.

Sólveig said:

> When I got home it seemed to me that more or less all the baby's brain was missing...You don't listen properly, maybe they do not tell you clearly enough, or maybe you cannot comprehend what you are being told. I remember the medical staff looking at books with pictures. I just lay there kind of numb. .. they [said]... can it be this or that?.. Leafing through, comparing pictures, getting out some more books, trying to figure this one out... I was lying there and [my husband] was sitting by me. It was as if we

were nothing. Then they sent us home. We went home, and decided to have the child, impairment or not. This was our child.

I probed further, wondering how they made the choice. Sólveig paused for a minute and then replied:

> I don't really know. This was always our child ... it was as if the medics were silly, I saw them as a bit stupid. We knew that this was our child, never mind what they said about it.

They were not given any specific advice by the doctors, but she thought that they expected them to have an abortion. When the parents returned to the hospital two days later they refused more tests because they feared that they would harm their unborn baby.

When the birth was due and they arrived at the hospital, they were asked whether they would mind if the birth was delayed so that some people could be present. They did not refuse. Then, the next morning the delivery room was lined with people in white coats.

Ólafur said:

> It was as if they expected a monster. I did not know what to say. Then the obstetrician entered. He looked around, obviously angry, and told everyone not directly involved to get out. That was a big relief...Then our daughter was born and looked beautiful, nothing like the children in the pictures...

These parents described their young daughter with great love and pride. At age 6, Vera could read and could not wait to start school. She had suffered a life-threatening illness, and been in and out of hospitals for almost four years, but got through that with excellent medical help. Life was again good to the small family. Yet the mother said that if she got into the same situation again she could not say beforehand what they would decide (i.e. whether to have a second child with impairment or not).

The context in which these data are anchored raises a number of questions. Why had the parents envisaged their unborn as a child, when the professionals saw only an impaired foetus? Did the fact that these parents already knew some people with disabilities who enjoyed their lives make a difference for their decision? Many more questions come to mind, but I argue that these data reflect contraries in peoples' perspectives, and that the individual/medical model, held inappropriately, caused the hurt and the clumsiness that the data lay bare. For Sólveig and Ólafur, their pregnancy was turned into a time of anxiety and fear for the future of their unborn child, and worries about whether or not they could cope as parents and as a couple. The actual birth became an undignified episode, a theatrical performance with a clinical lesson for the potential onlookers, and a deeply humiliating event for the parents. Things such as prenatal counselling are said to have improved since the mid 1990s, but these prospective parents' feelings of despair, dilemma and being rushed are still a major theme arising from the data.

Margrét had had fertility treatment and was expecting twins in the late 1990s. She knew in advance that one of them would most likely be significantly impaired, but that the other was not. Aborting one foetus would destroy the other. Because the couple was unlikely to be able to conceive again, they decided to go through with their pregnancy. These parents praised the medical services and support they received throughout after the diagnosis. When their child was born with multiple disabilities and significant health problems, the medical staff guided them through the maze of health and social services, ensured that they got whatever special service and financial support available, and some kept in contact with the family for years. Margrét described the doctor as "a true friend and a wonderful man. He supports us even now – and he has saved our family. I do not know what we would have done without him."

A different tale is told by Hrefna, the mother of Ásdís, a three-year-old girl with Down's syndrome, born in 2005. Hrefna and her husband Loftur, a seaman, already had two sons aged 12 and 8 and they wanted a daughter. Hrefna went for early ultrasound screening in the 14th week of pregnancy. Gunnar was at sea so she went alone. She was 38 years old. She had a hunch that something might be different with this child and had already discussed that possibility with her husband. They agreed to accept the child whatever the scan might reveal. When told that there might be something out of the ordinary with the foetus, that it might have Down's syndrome, they stuck to their initial decision. She had yet another scan taken in her second trimester, but no further tests. She spent some time researching what having a child with Down's syndrome could mean for them as a family, and turned to the website of the Down's Association, a parent association. She said:

> I realized that having a child with Down's syndrome was not the end of the world and that there was some help to be had for such a child if needed. We also both knew parents of a boy with Down's, a nice and happy family. We just went ahead preparing for our baby.

They were offered an abortion but felt no pressure. The doctor supported them and promised all the help the hospital could give. Loftur attended the birth. After the birth, they were given a private room. Loftur stayed with them all the time. He even slept there. Of course this couple had mixed feelings, and the pregnancy had been no bed of roses, but neither regrets their decision. She said: "We are happy with our little daughter, and her brothers are utterly in love with her".

As the examples above show clearly, the younger parents did not speak with one voice about their and their child's predicament during the prenatal period. But all the parents interviewed said that in retrospect they could not imagine their families without their disabled child. Most, nevertheless, acknowledged that they would make use of prenatal screening for their next pregnancy and possibly choose not to have a second impaired baby.

Those of the younger parents, the *Settlers* and the *Citizens* , who chose to give birth despite foetal difference, saw their choice as inevitable for them, and took the view that since society had given them the choice, society also had the responsibility of providing support for the consequences of that choice. The evidence also highlights the importance of having access to social capital, both bonding and bridging. I also interviewed parents from the *Settlers* and *The Citizens* groups who believed that they had "done everything according to the book"; obeyed their doctors, had the ultrasound, been given "a clean bill of health" for their prospective baby, only to have a disabled child. These parents certainly expressed their love and care for their child as did the other parents in this research. Nevertheless, the feeling of having "bought a damaged product" lingered, and these parents were the most likely to see their child's disability as a public issue.

STORIES OF ABORTIONS

Five of the couples interviewed had decided on the basis of the ultrasound results to have an abortion because of foetal difference. These stories differ depending on whether the prognosis indicated that the foetus could survive after birth or not, and on how the information about possible disability was delivered to the prospective parents.

Thora and Guðmundur, a couple with two children aged 6 and 10, live in a tiny, spartan flat in a suburb. Thora got pregnant by accident in 2006, but welcomed the pregnancy. She had a difficult medical problem and had to be operated on during her pregnancy. Her husband worried that the operation and subsequent treatment might have damaged the foetus, and suggested an abortion early on. Thora refused and he began to look forward to the new family member. Because of her illness, Thora was referred to several different specialists during the pregnancy, and their obstetrician saw her through. She said that he was their "anchor, and cared both about the illness and the "tiny one" [the word the couple used for their foetus]." Life changed at home. Thora spent a lot of time in hospital and Guðmundur was as often as possible at her side.

Their foetus did not develop as expected. Tests were taken and they had to wait for a few days for the result. That was hard. Thora said:

> The midwife had explained that if the problem was... [the genetic difference they suspected] I would be advised to have an abortion. The worst thing was that by this time I was so far gone. We had seen the "tiny one" many times; its brain was in place, the stomach, other organs, hands and feet. It had been moving for a while. Our children had been allowed to feel the kicking. They were happy and full of anticipation. ...There was milk in my breasts... For us the "tiny one" was not a foetus any more...

Guðmundur could not at first believe that something was seriously amiss. He concentrated on the thought that "he had to become hard as a rock for all of them". A few days later, the obstetrician asked them to come to the hospital. The test results confirmed that the foetus had the feared genetic difference, a life-threatening difference. It could not survive outside the mother's body. Guðmundur said:

> It was good that the doctor [they trusted] made the decision for us. He had the power, as a professional. He knew exactly what was happening, and he explained that the "tiny one" had no chance..

"We had no choice", said Thora, "It was either to finish this immediately or prolong the pain." For Thora "the hardest of all was to have to tell the children...but that could wait until after...". Three days later she had the abortion. In those three days Thora turned to her mother; she shut her husband out emotionally. "He just stood there and took what came, he did not know what to do or how to behave", she said. Her mother had to press her hard to remind her "that the 'tiny one' was also his". Guðmundur explained his reaction with the words: "The world collapsed. It was so fucking hard". He went home and carried on redecorating the kitchen.

When it was time for the abortion, the hospital staff were professional, but Thora did not feel that they showed compassion. Only one middle-aged woman orderly touched her hand and told her that it was "good to cry". For that she was grateful. The couple had been promised a private room both before and after the abortion. Thora wanted her husband by her side when she woke up. Neither plan worked out. She had sent her husband on errands. While in the mall he "felt as if I had turned to stone… I was outside myself, watching, like in a movie, it was surrealistic, all so strange…" He did not quite make it back in time. She woke up alongside other women in the same situation. The maternity ward was crowded. They were moved into a separate room which they had to share with a couple who also had undergone an abortion. Thora said:

> This was excruciating. It is a ward where teenage girls go for abortions. It is hard for a woman who does not want to lose her baby to be on the same ward. I felt angry at them and at my husband.

Later she found a silver lining. She told her husband that she was grateful that the "tiny one" was not found to have Down's syndrome or some similar non life-threatening problem. She explained:

> In such a case we would have had to make the really big decision on our own, a choice between life and death…before I always thought that if I got pregnant with a Down's syndrome child, I would have an abortion, now I realise that I could never do that.

Apart from the obstetrician who had supported them throughout, no other professional at the hospital stepped in to that role.

As a matter of course, they were asked if they wanted to see their foetus, and if they wanted to bury the ashes after its cremation. Thora wanted to do that, but Guðmundur refused. He told his wife: "If I get handed the urn with the ashes, and have to bury it, I will never get over this". At the time of the interview, life was getting back to a new routine. The children had not yet understood what had happened. The younger child was still angry and confused. Guðmundur was eager to try for a new baby as soon as possible but Thora was not so sure.

Apart from the obstetrician and Thora's mother, this young couple had little access to social capital of any kind for support. They came from different rural parts of the country, and both had left their childhood friends and most relatives behind when they met and married. They both told me that this experience had deepened their love for each other and their children. I believed them; their love for each other was almost tangible as we spoke.

The story of Atli and Ása is also about having an abortion, but it is a different story from the one above. Atli and Ása lived in a villa in a well-to-do suburb. They had three children aged from 3 to 14 years old, two of them from her previous marriage. Ása had a university education and a full time job; Atli owned a computer business. This was at the height of the economic boom in Iceland, and the couple worked long hours; he was some times away from home for weeks. They had recently bought the villa, changed its interior and refurnished it. They were starting a new life together, and there were loans to be paid off. Ása became pregnant in 2005. She and her husband went for her early ultrasound screening when she was in her 15th week of pregnancy. [3] The couple watched their foetus on the screen with anticipation. Suddenly the person operating the ultrasound scanner told them that "the nuchal fold" (soft marker nuchal thickening) did not look right. They did not understand, and looked at the screen in bewilderment. She then explained that this could indicate anything from a minor heart problem to something much more serious. An invasive diagnostic test could clarify the situation.

Ása said:

> The first thing that went through my head was "this will be OK. This is not the end of the world"… but my husband was badly shaken, perspired and wanted out of there.

Both felt that the scan operator directed her comments only to the prospective mother. Ása decided to send her husband home and wait alone for the test. Atli explained:

> I went numb, I had to be home and I could hardly talk. I am somewhere deep inside my own head sometimes in difficult situations.

They had talked about abortion before in a hypothetical manner, and knew each other's views. Atli's views were firm. He did not think that it should be within the power of people to decide who should be allowed to be born. He had been brought up to believe that an abortion due to foetal chromosomal difference was equivalent to murder. Ása was less sure about her views. This was, however, before they had to confront their personal dilemma.

---

[3] In early pregnancy, the phenomenon of nuchal translucency can be measured by obtaining an ultrasound scan. This technology has been promoted explicitly since the early 1990's as screening for Down's syndrome (Getz and Kirkengen, 2003).

Ásta got the test results by phone. She describes the phone call thus:

> It was early morning. I was at work. The doctor asked if he could talk to me there and then or if he should call later. For some reason I told him it was OK to talk. Then he said that the test results were not good... Down's syndrome. I cannot remember much more from the call. I returned to my work even though I could not concentrate...

They talked to an advisor at the hospital that same day. They felt they got woolly answers. They were informed about possible problems in general for a child with Down's, particularly about potential heart problems, hearing problems, developmental problems, shorter life expectancy, and problems with schooling and with leading a normal life. Atli felt himself to be "..an outsider in the conversation. Ása asked the questions and the consultants answered, I was just sitting there". He wished they had been given the opportunity to talk with a psychologist, preferably individually. They were also handed a brochure from the Down's Association and urged to go and see people there. They leafed through the brochure but decided not to go. Ása researched on the internet. What she read scared her, "...it was all so negative", she said, "even when parents are writing about their own children, the negative by far outweighs the positive". They decided to tell no-one immediately, and to make the decision by themselves. Somehow they did not find time in their busy schedules to talk about this for a while. Ásta thought for a time that she would have the baby, but as she collected more information from different [medical model] sources, her views changed. She also consulted a woman friend who had had an abortion. When she had more or less made up her mind to have the abortion she suggested to Atli that they should call his uncle, a spiritual medium. Atli said:

> I called him, ... I was greatly relieved and called him several times about this. He did not tell us what to do, but supported whatever decision we would make. As long as it was a foetus, the decision was ours. Then he said a sentence that I will always remember. He said: let your feelings, not rational thought lead you...Let your heart decide...This encouraged me to want to keep the child.

They both struggled over the decision for three weeks. He struggled with his conscience, his religious beliefs and doubts. Ása's thoughts were with their other children. Why should they put them through the experience of having a disabled sibling? They would be teased, even bullied, and have their quality of life reduced.

> We would have less time for them and… I was much more concerned about them than us. I was also worried about the kind of a life the unborn child would have…

She also worried whether or not they would have to move to a different house, and if they could keep their jobs, if this child was born. When I asked her where she thought all these difficult ideas came from, she did not know. She said: "probably from my childhood, but maybe the consultation at the hospital had something to do with it". Ása finally made up her mind to have an abortion. Atli said:

> We decided this together. I support her all the way, but I am still not happy with the decision. .. but I might not have been happy with a different decision either. I will probably never fully accept the decision we made…

When the doctor called Ása at work to ask what they had decided, his reaction was unexpected. She said:

> It was strange. He sounded angry on the phone and asked me: Do you know what this means? Then he turned ice cold and clinical and explained the procedure at hand. All this went on over the phone [at work]…he did not invite us to come and speak with him directly…I cried at my desk, I cried in the car and when I picked our youngest up from his preschool…It was so difficult to see all these little children at the preschool every day…so terribly difficult…

Ásta was also worried about other people's opinion. She said: "Maybe people will think us evil to do something like this". They told their nearest family members about it two days before the abortion, and Atli told his childhood friend. Both found support from their mothers and closest family, but it was harder for Atli's friend to accept. He and his wife were expecting a baby. That strained their friendship.

They were finally called to the hospital to sign papers and talk with the consultant and the doctor. Little was said. They signed the papers, were asked why they had taken this decision, got to choose between two dates for the operation and then left. They opted for the earliest possible date. The abortion was performed at the maternity ward of the hospital, where they were surrounded by pregnant women, new mothers and babies. Ása found that peculiar and difficult. Her husband was at her side and they got a private room. Two days later it was over. After the abortion, they were invited to see the foetus.

Atli said:

> I will never regret that. I stayed with the "tiny one"…It was difficult, but something I needed to do. I needed to show it all my warmth and respect.

The staff were professional. Ása and Atli were given phone numbers to call if they needed psychological help. They asked to speak to a clergyman. He talked to them a few times. At their request he helped to get their foetus buried. With the permission of the relatives of a deceased elderly woman they had not known, the foetus was put in the coffin with her (this is a common custom in Iceland). They were told that the dead woman had been a good person. That way, they have a grave they can visit. This, Atli explained "calms the soul". Sometimes they light a candle for their unborn child at home. They do not talk much about their ordeal. Atli occupies himself at work. Two weeks after the abortion Ásta was contacted by hospital staff and asked how they were doing. She was urged to call the ward whenever she needed to, and again offered psychological help. The clergyman called, offered help and invited them to contact him. Ásta was grateful for this, but did not think such support was necessary. Her boss at work had also been informed about what had happened, was sympathetic and gave her time off on full pay.

REFLECTIONS

The younger parents, the *Settlers* and the *Citizens*, were forced by the technology, the *zeitgeist* and their personal experiences and perspectives to make difficult choices. Some "did everything right" according to the prenatal medical blueprint only to have a child with disability, others had to choose between having a disabled child, bearing a child that could not survive and watching it die, or terminating the pregnancy of an impaired foetus that could have lived. Contrast this with the fate of the *Explorers* and the *Pioneers*, the parents who got the child Fate, God or luck gave them. For the younger parents even the question whether or not to allow a disabled child to be born was becoming a public issue. Parents' wishes were respected when firm, but if they were hesitant, they were made to think about schooling, special services, cost, and so on, even before they met their unborn child.

In making their choices, they were heavily dependent upon information, advice and support. Many of these parents had little informal support from friends or relatives. Most did not know any disabled people who lived a good life in harmony with their families and friends. Furthermore, the professional support and advice they received was mostly from people trained to think and work along the lines of the medical model perspective. Many supplemented that information by sources on the internet, often sources provided by medical experts. I ask myself if these stories would have turned out differently if these parents had received substantial informal support from relatives and friends, advice from experts from the social model perspective, or if they had known persons with disabilities from their schooling or other parts of their lives.

The Icelandic health services are thought to be amongst the best and most comprehensive in the world. The health statistics confirm this (Hagstofa Íslands, e.d.a). These services are more costly to the state and the taxpayer than any other single service in the country. The main hospitals are highly technological. The staff are professional, well trained, and experienced. Much of the staff are also presumably kind people who opted for their line of work out of compassion for others. The data show clearly that the parents treasure every little kind word or deed experienced during their ordeals. So how can it be that in situations like those described above, situations in which the parents or prospective parents are highly vulnerable, there seems to be at times so little tact? Is that simply something lost in the busy work schedule at the hospital, or has it something to do with the disability issues in focus?

DEALING WITH ASSESSMENT

Every family in the *Settlers* and the *Citizens* groups reported obtaining services for their disabled child or children from the SDCC (State Diagnostic and Counselling Centre). Initial diagnosis was given by general practitioners, specialists, medical teams at hospitals, psychologists, psychiatrists, the National Centre for Hearing and Speech Impairment, and even special educators at a preschool or school; but almost all children seen to be in need of special support due to a developmental or behavioural difference were also diagnosed and labelled by the SDCC[4]. The label has become a necessity, a ticket to help in any shape or form. This applies equally to the right to support in school or preschool, disability grants, technical aids, free nappies and so on. Since the establishment of the SDCC in 1986, new laws have replaced older legislation and enabled its expansion and restructuring. On the home page of the SDCC it states that:

> The most important of these are the 1992 legislation on the Affairs of the Disabled and the current legislation on the State Diagnostic and Counselling Centre from 2003 (Lög um Greiningar- og ráðgjafarstöð ríkisins. nr. 83/2003). Since 1991 the SDCC has expanded, increased its specialisation, added new experts, new services to parents and children with disability (aged 0-18 years), created a much clearer organisational structure and attracted significant increase in funding. SDCC co-operation with relevant bodies at both state and municipal levels has expanded and become more systemic. It also has expanded its educational and research side significantly. In the 1980s approximately 100 referrals were made to the SDCC per year, in 1998 that number had grown to approximately 200 per year, in 2004 the number climbed to just below 300, and in 2008 referrals were 344 (Greiningar- og ráðgjafarstöð ríkisins, e.d.b). [5]

Thus the SDCC has become the major "producer" of children seen to have a difference in body or mind, into diagnosed subjects (Jóhannesson, 2006), or social artefacts (Allan, 1999) composing a residual category of "them" rather than "us". At the SDCC, the definition of disability is firmly based on a medical model definition as in ICD-10 (World Health Organization, 1992, 1993). The ICD-11 (World Health Organization, 2001, 2006) is known to the staff of the SDCC but it does not yet form the basis for their definition of disability. That newer version, even though still based on medical model thinking, pays greater attention to social factors and social domains interplaying with the diagnosis.

---

[4]Other organisations entrusted with formal diagnosis are BUGL (a part of Landspítali, the University hospital, services for children and youth with mental health and developmental problems), the Centre for Hearing and Speech Impairment and the Centre for Visual Impairment. Frequently these organisations work alongside or in co-operation with the SDCC when children are being assessed for impairment.

[5]On the home page of the SDCC it also says: The main problems of children 0-18 years of age referred to the SDCC are mental retardation, autism, physical impairment and blindness. The SDCC also engages in research and education in co-operation with national and international organisations in these fields.

The SDCC estimates that about 3.5% of each cohort of children will need its services in the near future[6]. These arguments and estimates, along with the waiting list (which for some reason always remains long, how ever much money the government puts into the SDCC kitty) can be seen as an effort by the SDCC to improve the lot of disabled children. But it could also be taken to indicate a culture of empire-building, of pushing its "mystical diagnostic know-how", and of seeking expansion of staff and resources. It is unclear, for example, why labels that appear to be easily certifiable by local experts such as teachers, doctors or psychologists, are required to be certified by the SDCC, as are differences that schools are for the most part well equipped to deal with.

Since 1990 there has been an increase in referrals of children thought to be on the autism spectrum, particularly amongst younger age groups. This is partly due to a change in diagnostic definitions (Greiningar- og ráðgjafarstöð ríkisins, e.d.b). A similar trend has been noted in many other western countries and is partly unexplained (Dillenburger, et al., 2010). In Iceland, children diagnosed on the autism spectrum as a proportion of all births 1984-1993 were estimated at 13.2/10,000 whereas the equivalent figure for 1974-1983 was 4.2/10,000 (Greiningar- og ráðgjafarstöð ríkisins, e.d.b). Changes in knowledge, technology and diagnostic methods, more resources including expert staff, and increased life expectancy of premature babies are amongst the explanations given as to why the services of the SDCC have been steadily extended.

---

[6]The home page of the SDCC defines its prospective clients thus:....Generally it is estimated that approx. 15-20% of all children need support due to a health problem/and or learning problems in their childhood or youth, and that approx. 3% of all children have such serious problems, that they are likely to need support in their everyday life in adulthood. It is advisable to estimate that 3.5% of each age cohort of children attend the SDCC each year or approx. 160 children and young people, and 4500 children in each age cohort. Within that frame will be children with intellectual impairment, children with autism/disorders on the autism spectrum and children with serious mobility problems/blindness/visual impairment. Also children with mixed and complex disorders/ and or serious supplementary disorders, in need of services in 3 degree level institutions.

In order to obtain this goal, the following is estimated:
a) Children with mental retardation - IQ $\leq$65 (1% = 45 children in each age group)
b) Children with autism/ disorders on the autism spectrum (1% = 45 children in each age group)
c) Children with serious mobility problems and /or blindness/visual impairment (0.5% = 22 children in each age group)
d) Children with IQ 65-70 and/or mixed/complex disorders and /or serious supplementary disorders (1% =45 children in each age group).

More children might be added because of serious neglect/ abuse and violence, serious hearing impairment, or because parents have mental retardation/special needs and/ or a complex cultural or language environment. In addition children with rare disorders such as Retts disorder, developmental atrophy, Landau-Kleffner syndrome, or acquired brain damage.

The younger parents in the *Settlers* and the *Citizens* groups did not speak with one voice about their experiences of the SDCC any more than did the parents in the older groups. Most of these parents, however, were grateful for the services they received, particularly the support and advice from social workers.

Grímur, a farmer, was the father of Birna, a girl born in 1999 and diagnosed with autism and a genetic abnormality. Grímur was no newcomer to the disability service system. His sister had been diagnosed with the same disorder in the late 1960s, and was moved to an institution before her eighth birthday. Grímur's father spearheaded the *Explorers'* parent movement in his community. Grímur had lived most of his childhood and youth with a father who spent almost all his spare time on disability issues, pushing for changes in laws, regulations and systems, including the improvement of assessment services. Grímur's mother managed much of the everyday work on the farm, visited his older sister a few times a year, brought her home occasionally for Christmas and holidays, but hardly mentioned her in between.

Grímur had married his childhood sweetheart, Anna, when they were in their teens. Financially, things were hard, and they had almost nobody to turn to; their closest neighbours were relatives of Anna's, but they objected to having Birna visit them, and communications with that part of the extended family were broken. Her sister, who lived in another town, sometimes helped out. Life was very tough for the family. When Grímur was told that he had transmitted the genetic difference to his only child, he could not face it at first. He said: "I did not want to turn into my dad and ruin the life of my wife…". After having a vasectomy and going through a difficult time with his family, he came to terms with his daughter's difference. He explained his experience of the SDCC:

> Ironically we were harvesting what my father and others had planted. The SDCC is a fine organisation with several experts, a hierarchy and defined ways of working. But Birna had to wait two years for the diagnosis from the SDCC. She had a diagnosis from our doctors, of course. When her turn came [at the SDCC], they were fine and did a nice job I think. But somehow I do not understand why the main diagnosis was necessary, we knew what she had.

But his wife, Anna had a very different tale to tell. She said:

> We only got to know what the matter was after the diagnosis at the SDCC, when she was two years old. Her problems are to do with developmental delay, mobility, sight and possibly hearing…and autism. The

staff [at the SDCC] were great, particularly the social worker, who supported me, asked me how I was doing, and the physiotherapist, a genius who could get Birna to do amazing things... she taught me how to handle her.

Almost all the parents defined the services they got from the SDCC as an issue of *rights* which their disabled children were entitled to under the law. Many were apprehensive, reporting both positive and negative experiences at the SDCC, and with varying accounts of the extent to which they and their children got the support from the SDCC that they were entitled to.

Finally, a few parents, like some of those in the older groups, expressed surprise and anger at some of the tests given to their children in the unfamiliar surroundings of the SDCC, and the sweeping conclusions drawn from them, and for having to wait for services for their child for months. From these parents' points of view, however, appreciation of the support received from the SDCC increased with time. Parents who lived out in the country were especially appreciative of the staff at the SDCC who visited them or called them on a regular basis, and consulted with their child's school or preschool. Overall, more parents from amongst the *Citizens* were pleased with the services of the SDCC than parents from the other groups. This holds especially true when the child's disability label did not imply very complex difference and consequently complex solutions. Thus parents of a child with Down's syndrome and no additional problems were amongst those most pleased with the services and support, but parents of children on the autism spectrum were the least satisfied. Parents of disabled children who lived in some of the experimental municipalities and experienced successful co-operation between professionals employed by their municipality and the SDCC experts were the most pleased of all the parents with the services they received. However, the reasons given by parents in the two younger groups, the *Settlers* and the *Citizens*, for their appreciation, concern or anger were somewhat different from those given by parents in the older groups. The older parents commented on individual professionals at Kjarvalshús and later at the early SDCC. Kjarvalshús was praised for its warm, homely atmosphere, the good coffee and individualised attention. The professionals were all named and remembered. They were praised for their kindness, compassion, willingness to travel, and for teaching the parents and others new ways to help the disabled child. These same professionals were by others blamed for clumsiness in interaction, for reading too much or too little into tests, or for stating the obvious.

The younger parents focused more on the *team* of experts and their work. Often they could not name a single individual professional, except maybe the medical doctor who had been most important for them and their child. Occasionally, they remembered the first name of a SDCC professional who had been notably helpful or clumsy.

Katrín and Viktor, the parents of Vera, the little girl who was not expected to live used the disability services as little as possible at first. That changed after the SDCC diagnostic process, where they met specialists who believed that their daughter could survive. Katrín said:

> We are happy with what support we have. The first year we did not expect her to live, so we took one day at the time…Later we went to see her neurologist, and took her to the institute for the blind… A social worker there took us on… she and another social worker from the SDCC help us. [The latter] is kind and able and we know her name… it is Gudrún something… She calls us to meetings, informs us, and co-ordinates the help our daughter is entitled to. She asks us what we want, points out different solutions, hears what we say and respects our daughter…Both these social workers have been excellent, particularly Gudrún. There is nothing she is not willing to do for our girl. She must believe that she is going to survive…

Some were not even sure about the name of the doctor working with their child at the SDCC. This was especially common if that doctor did not enter the picture outside the SDCC, before or after the diagnosis. As before, the final diagnosis was both welcomed by the parents as a relief from the period of uncertainty, but often came also as a shock. Amongst the *Citizens*, parents of children diagnosed by the SDCC as being on the autism spectrum admitted to returning home scared and confused. One father summed up what many parents in that situation felt. He said:

> Why is this all so complex – no clear answers to why this happened to our child, and no clear solutions? He is our son, but his problem is not ours alone. He has his rights, and the SDCC should help more. After all we pay for that through our taxes.

DEALING WITH THE SSI

The younger parents, like the older parents, found it difficult dealing with the SSI to get grants, technical aids and so on, which they believed (or knew) that their disabled child and family were entitled to under the law. The bureaucratic rules were in place for these parents, but often complex, with the chain of requests, applications and complaints long and confusing. One father described dealing with the system (SSI) as "an additional disability placed on the family". He said "the system has grown and become a kind of a monster, and to crack it you need several university degrees". Despite the exaggeration, this echoes the views of several parents interviewed for this study. A single mother gave her views on the SSI thus:

> I am too stupid to figure all this out. At times I am also too tired to deal with the paperwork at night, after my day's work, housework and putting the children to bed. Sometimes I simply give up, at other times I ask a lawyer friend to help. I do not know why this should be so confusing. I am normally not considered stupid, with my university degree and all.

And a man who directs a large firm, the father of a child with complex needs born in 1999, said:

> All this form-filling rubbish is typical for the incompetence of state-run services. I have given up, I have no time for this business. We simply buy the technical aids he needs.

Furthermore, with societal and lifestyle changes in Iceland, the parents' perspectives on what their disabled children needed changed. For example, a disabled child with many, often heavy technical aids, was seen by parents to be in need of some duplicate aids, but under the SSI regulations the taxpayer only paid for one set. These parents were tired of moving the stuff between home and school, or, if the parents were separated or divorced, between their homes.

Grímur, the father of Birna, said:

> I grew up with my father's fights with the SSI, and knew that dealing with them is no picnic. They always use the same tactic. That did not surprise me. Once we sent them a formal complaint, because they downgraded Birna's diagnostic label, which meant that we were entitled to a lower grant for her care than before. It took months to put right; letters, phone calls, trips to Reykjavík and endless copies of reports and medical certificates. Later they refused to give us a voucher for free nappies. That time we got the social worker at the SDCC to help us. She cleared that for us with the SSI, no problem...

The pain, irritation and sense of humiliation reported by the parents resulting from such bureaucratic struggles were intense. The parents, especially the *Citizens*, were often devastated by what they felt was a failure of the state to uphold or respect their and their child's basic human rights. Some tried to carry on the struggle with the SSI with whatever means, orthodox and unorthodox, they had at their disposal, but for the most part complaints were in vain. Others simply gave up, and still others used their access to social capital, a friend, a relative, an MP, whatever political or bureaucratic contact they could dredge up, to ensure that their application got processed in a satisfactory way.

Medical model perspectives are to a large extent at the core of the definitions of entitlement. This has not changed much since 1974. What has changed is the sum of the taxpayer's money the state has allocated to the SSI to support disabled children, together with the provisions of special grants, technological and other aids which these parents can apply for[7]. Such support has improved, and become more widely available free of charge. But the child must fit distinct categories of diagnosis under the rules.

Compared with the older parents, there has been a tremendous improvement in the provision of formal support to disabled children in the younger families. Further, as mentioned before, the SSI still pays hospital bills and travel costs for a child and one parent when the child needs a life-saving operation in a high-technology hospital abroad. However, the bureaucratic blueprint is inflexible, and individual families frequently find themselves as square pegs trying to fit round holes. They tend to find that, despite the fact that important support from the SSI exists *de jure*, their family or child does not fit the criteria. The struggle with the SSI is for many parents a struggle for their child's human rights (Bjarnason, 2010). The state support distributed by the SSI is seen as self-evident, as a *rights* issue, and the struggle a public issue.

DEALING WITH EDUCATION

The *Settlers'* children had by law, and increasingly in practice, access to education and special support at school, both in ordinary schools and preschools, and in special classes in ordinary compulsory schools (Marinósson, 2007). Access to special schools was (and still is) available to

---

[7] I have not been able to get at the exact figures. They are hard to extract from the overall outgoings of the SSI, but its total budget paid out has increased significantly over the years (Herbertsson, 2005; Ólafsson, 2005).

disabled children with families living in or near Reykjavík and (for a while and now again), in Akureyri in the north.

Since Iceland signed the Salamanca declaration in 1994 the Ministry of Education has made some effort to implement it in compulsory education. As we have seen, the educational system underwent changes in the 1990s which opened up access to regular schooling for disabled children. All the preschools in the land now accept (at least formally) disabled children in regular classes, and what special units there were have been closed down. This may be changing, as the parent lobby for children labelled with autism is currently lobbying for new special units for their children ("Deild fyrir einhverf börn," 2009).

Integration and, by the middle of the 1990s, *inclusive education* became buzzwords in educational policy and, slowly, in practice. There was still, however, a great deal of resistance to including disabled children in many schools, particularly schools in the urban area. The arguments against including a particular disabled child included lack of resources, teaching skills, the architecture of the school or playground, overburdened teachers and lack of staff. Parents sometimes had to listen to these arguments when they applied to a school to enrol their disabled child. In the latter half of the 1990s upper secondary schools were gradually expected to provide educational opportunities for disabled youngsters, and many opened up special units for students with intellectual impairment. Parents from among the *Settlers* became the horse that pulled the wagon of that particular change.

The mother of Valur, a boy who was born in a rural area in 1996 and uses a wheelchair, described their struggle with the local school thus:

> I always know exactly what my child costs the school. The headmaster makes a point of telling me each year, and how many children with ordinary special needs could be taught for that money. I know that [Valur] is expensive, but we have no special schools and it's his right to be at school with his siblings and neighbours. Each year the two municipalities that share the running cost of our school argue about which one should pay for his extra needs, for alterations to the school building, putting in ramps and altering the WC for his use. For a long time nothing happened – they simply carried him from A to B. The local Area Board for the Disabled has not been helpful [in putting this right]. My husband and I have repeatedly asked them to make the school accessible. They have sent polite letters, but nothing happens. We had to push; first the preschool and then at the local school [for them to do this]. Valur needs physical support and some special education because of his dyslexia, but it is hard for us to control how that is done. He sometimes

comes home unhappy and wet, because no one had time to help him use the bathroom. Still, many of the teachers are kind and they help him even when it is not part of their job…

Valur's mother grew tired of waiting for the Area Board officers, the preschool teachers and the compulsory school staff to set up a joint planning meeting before Valur started in his local school. She decided to call these people to a meeting herself. She even found a support person for Valur at school. That person has since been hired by the school to support Valur and a few other children in need of assistance. Valur is the first child in his school with significant impairment and his parents have had to "struggle all the way" to get him necessary support, but Valur happens to be strong both socially and educationally (except for the dyslexia) and is on the whole doing well at school. He has a number of friends there who help him at times and enjoy his company.

Similar stories are told by many of the other parents in the *Settlers* group. Most often the preschools were reported as open and accessible to disabled children, and many parents expressed their delight in dealing with preschool staff. But the transition from preschool to school was often problematic. Many parents felt that they had to struggle with ordinary schools in order to get their child necessary personal support, to get adaptations made to the buildings and playgrounds, and to get different professional parties to communicate. Many also reported that they were uncertain about whether or not the teaching methods were appropriate or if the demands made on their child were adequate. Most reported that their children gradually became isolated from friends and classmates as they moved into their teens, and began to feel isolated and lonely at that time. This was one of the parents' greatest worries. These findings coincide with a recent study on the schooling of all Icelandic children with intellectual impairment (Marinósson, 2007).The parents in the *Citizens* group inherited the changes in educational law and practice. As I write, their children are still at preschool or the lower years of compulsory school. Most of these parents expect inclusive schooling for their disabled children, or special classes at their local schools, but with necessary and sufficient support to access learning, friends and the school community.

Some parents amongst the *Citizens* elect to enroll their disabled children into a special school. The reasons given for this are: they do not trust the regular school; their local school does not really accept the disabled child, with the headmaster highlighting all the problems involved; they do not believe that ordinary schools have the special skills and competence to deal with their child's significant needs; they fear that their child will not make any friends in the ordinary school, due to the developmental gap between their child and the non-labelled students, and expect their child to find company amongst others "like him or her". Finally there were parents who stated clearly, that due to the pressure of their work, the special school with added-on services was the only option for them and their disabled child and family. These are the parents who have started to voice their concerns and lobby for new special schools (Þorláksson, et al., 2008). They also complain that children at special schools are being dismissed as a residual category by the inclusion lobby, due to its lack of understanding of the severity of those children's special needs, and the extraordinary pressure their parents have to live with. Medical model professionals, including the staff at the SDCC and some special teachers and bureaucrats, appear to support this claim. Politicians in the Reykjavík City Council, with its recent right wing/neoliberal leadership, have shown interest in building a new special school, reversing its former policy on inclusion, and such a school was on the drawing board when these plans were put on hold following the economic collapse in 2008.

Still, inclusive education has become the norm in Icelandic schools and preschools, at least in theory. According to our 2007 study *Tálmar og tækifæri*, staff at all school levels expressed positive attitudes towards children with intellectual impairment. These include: the belief that all children and young people can learn, that they are entitled to appropriate support at school, entitled to active participation in their school and society, and that they should be subjected to equity and social justice (Marinósson, 2007). Staff attitudes also reflect the view that schools are obliged to provide students who have intellectual disability with appropriate learning tasks, and that they should attend to those students' learning needs with the same diligence as with all other students (Marinósson, 2007). In many schools, however, special teachers spend a significant amount of time with one or a few students with special educational needs who have been pulled out of regular class lessons.

Once the disabled child is in school, whether it be an ordinary compulsory education school (included or in a special class) or a special school, parents, at least those of children with intellectual impairment, say that they are pleased with their child's schooling. This was also shown in our study, *Tálmar og tækifæri* (Marinósson, 2007), which investigated the schooling of all Icelandic students with intellectual impairment. Parents of disabled children labelled with intellectual impairment who attended compulsory and upper secondary schools filled in questionnaires where they were asked about their satisfaction with their child's school. Most parents said they were satisfied and believed that their child's school and teachers were doing a good job. It emerged, however, that many of these parents knew very little about what actually happened in school. It also emerged that teachers were largely satisfied with their disabled students, but that in regular schools teachers commonly left the planning and specialised teaching to the special educator, and that disabled students spent most of their time with unskilled teaching assistants (Marinósson, 2007).

These data show that, although inclusive education has become the norm in Icelandic preschools and compulsory schools (only 0.4% of labelled children are in special schools), the quality of educational and social provision may be less clear. Despite stating general satisfaction with their children's schooling, be it special or regular (as did parents in the study *Tálmar og tækifæri*), the younger parents in this study still encountered obstacles when trying to secure educational services for their children. They felt they needed to struggle for their children's acceptance into generic schools, for appropriate generic or specialised educational services and equipment, and, hardest of all, to get their older disabled children accepted by peers and friends. A few parents opted for special schools, and complained that the political emphasis on inclusion had left their children out, diminished and demeaned their significant special needs, and blocked resources for the extra and complex care they needed. As before, the younger parents do not speak in one voice. Finally, there is some indication that the special school lobby may be gaining ground, as shown by the massive popular interest in the exhibition *Exceptional Children* at the National Museum of Iceland in September 2007 to February 2008. This exhibition showed photographs from two Icelandic special schools by Mary Ellen Mark, a distinguished photographer who has specialised in photographing outsiders and marginalised people around the world. Featuring pictures of children as objects of pity (Mark, Hallgrímsdóttir, and Ingólfsson, 2007), the exhibition drew large crowds, stirred the public debate on inclusive versus special schooling, and highlighted the claim of some parents and teachers of children in special schools (Sigurðardóttir, 2009; Þorláksson, et al., 2008) that Iceland needed a new and modernised special school.

Chapter 6

THE FATHERS

Fathers and mothers were interviewed separately for this study if at all possible. For some reason it was harder to get interviews with fathers than with mothers; they forgot the set time, were called away because of their jobs or errands, or they believed that it was enough for me to talk to their wife or partner, because she would be better able to answer my questions about their disabled child or children. "She is the skipper on the family boat", "she deals with most of that stuff", or "she deals with all the professionals and does the phone-work", they told me. Of the 75 families I got interviews with 51 fathers, and of those 9 were interviewed together with their wife or partner at the couple's request.

As I began to listen to the fathers voices alone, new questions came to mind. Their stories were not the same as the stories told by their wives or partners, and many of their stories were being told for the first time in these interviews. They were stories of deep love and concern for their children and their partners, stories about being in denial and sorrow because of their child's disability, stories of helplessness, bravery, anger and resilience, and of loneliness and isolation. And there were many stories that began with the sentence, "I realised that I had to be strong for all of us". As I listened I asked myself how the fathers perceived the available support (both formal and informal), who supported them, and to what extent the changes in formal support and social policy over the years affected their perception of having a child with disability. Focusing on the fathers' roles, I also wondered whether they experienced their tasks vis-à-vis the family and work in a different way from the mothers.

The study highlights the fact that it was mostly the mothers who dealt with support systems, both formal and informal, even when the fathers took time out to attend meetings at the SDCC, the preschool or school. Mothers mostly dealt with both his and her extended family and friends; they decided, from amongst both their extended families and friends, who should be told what, whom to ask or accept help from, and even who should be invited in or kept at a distance. Fathers would sometimes come along to a meeting to add weight to their wives' arguments or requests, ask the hard questions, or simply to listen, learn and show solidarity with the child and family. Fathers in all the age groups were less likely than the mothers to go to meetings in connection with disability issues, or attend courses. When fathers attended such events, they were likely to leave early. Several fathers explained to me that they preferred to stay at home and look after the children, let their wives go to these events, and then learn from them about the particular course or meeting. The wives or partners also mostly dealt with the professionals, from infant swimming teachers and physiotherapists, to staff at the respite, the preschools, the schools and other services. The women attended all the meetings if they possibly could, helped set up schedules, organised, did a lot of the paperwork, did exercises with their disabled child, dealt with homework and so on. The women also took on much of the care-giving role in their families. On the whole, it was the women who decided where to send a disabled child to school and preschool, if there was any question of choice. They also had the last word on whether or not a foetus diagnosed with an abnormality should be born or aborted. Mostly, of course, they did this in concert with their partners or husbands, and kept them informed. Almost all the mothers also had jobs outside the family, part or full time, and a few couples were dual career families, with both husband and wife engaged in taxing professional work. Obviously there were exceptions to this. In two families interviewed, for example, the father dealt with many such issues. In one case this was so because the mother was an invalid, in the other case because the father said he needed to be in control. In addition, there were several couples who apparently did all these things together without dividing the labour; this applied particularly to the two lesbian couples included in the study. All but two of the fathers were fully employed or ran their own businesses. They included bankers, businessmen of medium and small firms, professional men, skilled and unskilled workers, fishermen and farmers. Two fathers were on invalid pension; the rest of them tended to work long hours, from 9 to 12 hours per day, and most also did some work at week-ends. A number of the fathers had two jobs, and a few were migrant workers.

So what do these fathers do in their roles as fathers and husbands? The evidence shows that most fathers supported the mothers in their struggle for services and entitlements for their disabled child or children, even if they did not always agree with the mothers' definitions of what the children's special needs were. Peter, the father of Kristín, in the second vignette of this book, felt that his wife Mary was over-anxious, wanting him to learn about Kristín's disability too quickly, and that once the struggle for services started in earnest, everything moved too fast for him. He felt that his wife's struggle demanded that he turned his life around. He was also not always sure that Kristín needed all the services his wife thought essential. Still, he supported her the best he could, and admired her for her stamina. The story of Atli's terrible dilemma is another case in point. He consented to his wife having an abortion and supported her through it, ridden with doubts he tried to conceal. He saved his marriage at the cost of agreeing to the abortion of a foetus that might have been born with Down's syndrome.

The fathers took on "viscosious roles" in the home and family (Goodley, 2007), gravitating towards tasks that the mothers gave them or could not deal with. They provided care to the disabled child, lifting, carrying and bathing their children with mobility problems as they grew heavier, if they happened to be at home. They also looked after their other children when the mother was away or unable to do so. They tried (with varying success) to listen to the mothers, and did practical work such as some housework, "taxi driving" for family members, and most supervised the maintenance of home and family car. A few of the older fathers went as far as building ramps, and fixing doors or bathrooms in their disabled children's preschools and schools. Some, but not all, involved themselves in major disputes with the school authorities or wrote letters to administrators at the SSI. Some fathers living in rural areas undertook to drive their disabled child to and from school and other local services each day, when the relevant authorities failed to provide such services. It is also clear from the data that those fathers who could claim access to bridging and linking social capital, through party political membership, kinship, old school friends or other such connections, used that to solicit help for their disabled child, something they might have hesitated to do in other circumstances.

Several fathers in the sample observed that most of the professionals they met in meetings to do with their child's disability were female. This made some of them uncomfortable, feeling awkward with their masculinity; this is particularly noticeable in the older fathers' narratives and in interviews with manual workers and fishermen. Other fathers had a completely different view and said they were used to working with women and found them easier to talk to than their male counterparts. Several fathers, from both the older and younger groups, commented that in meetings they sometimes felt invisible, as if the professionals directed attention and words at the mothers, and that their (the fathers') questions were not heard or remained unanswered unless they made an effort to attract the professionals' attention. A father from the *Settlers* group expressed his experience thus:

> I see no reason to go to all these meetings. My wife goes. She tells me what happened when she gets back. I went to meetings at the SDCC a few times. I felt almost invisible; apart from the doctor I was the only man there, and even he spoke mainly to my wife. He addressed us as "you" [in the plural], but somehow I was shy to ask questions and did not want to interfere. So now I mostly stay behind and take care of things here...

Most of the fathers found it hard to combine their working lives, their roles as fathers and husbands, and tasks related to parent/professional encounters.

A few fathers helped develop or organise services for disabled people, either by participating in local politics, or by joining or organising local parent groups of disabled children connected to the parent association, *Þroskahjálp,* or the older organisation, *Styrktarfélag vangefinna*. Grímur, who belongs to the *Citizens* and has a six-year-old daughter with autism and a genetic abnormality, had passed this onto her and found this an almost unbearable fact to accept. He fell severely depressed and retreated into denial, which almost broke his marriage. When he recovered and faced what had happened, he became one of the leading parent activists in his area.

Grímur's father, a powerful and determined man, had thrown himself into the fight for improving services for disabled people in the area. He was a member of the most powerful political party in the region, and could put pressure on government ministers and local politicians. He was away a lot, dealing with advocacy and other local issues. He sat on boards and committees, and helped build the local and national disability service system under the legislation of 1979 (Lög um aðstoð við þroskahefta nr. 47/1979). He had little time to spare for his family. As a teenager, Grímur rebelled against this, and swore never to participate in any political or public service activities. Now as an adult, he feels that his generation of parents is reaping the benefits of his father's efforts. But also, to his dismay, he feels that he "is turning into his father", involving himself with politics and local disability affairs.

Very few fathers reported having trusted male friends with whom they could talk about private matters. Perhaps this is a part of the masculine make-up in Iceland and probably elsewhere. This does not mean that the fathers said they did not have friends, or that their friends did not show compassion for their predicament. Those fathers who said that they had been supported by a friend were likely to mention a woman friend if they needed someone to talk to, but male friends in the context of practical support, such as help to build ramps, paint or do other home maintenance or mend cars. One father told a story of his mates bringing the family a washing machine and bottle of vodka, pretending that the visit had been all about drinking the vodka. The most often mentioned help from mates or bosses was being given flexibility at work, to take time off when their disabled child or family needed help. For example, a fisherman who was told that his wife had just given birth to a disabled baby appreciated that he was immediately given time off "for as long as he needed it". When he rejoined his crew, however, no one mentioned the baby or that he had just become a father. And a teacher from the *Settlers* group said: "I could talk to my friends about what was happening, but not about how I felt".

A few of the fathers in the *Citizens* group had a very different tale to tell. Thor, Danni's father, from the third vignette in this book, called an older male friend who had a child with Down's syndrome almost immediately after the birth of his son. They had a long conversation, which helped Thor to come quickly to terms with their new situation, and enabled him to take charge and give strength and protection to his wife and their extended family members. That story is unique in the data, but other evidence shows that the younger fathers were a bit more able to share their thoughts and feelings with trusted friends (mostly childhood friends) than their older counterparts. However, many of the fathers from all the groups said that they did not have real friends apart from the wife.

None of the fathers reported that the professionals directed support at them as persons. Many did not expect any such support, because "this is about our child, not about me" (as one father put it), but there were also several fathers who said that it would have been good to talk matters over with some professional outside their family – "like a male psychologist" at the SDCC. Many fathers also reported getting little or no personal support from their own relatives. Almost two thirds of the fathers interviewed said they got no or little such support; those who did said that they could speak to their parents (mostly mothers), a sister or occasionally a brother about their concerns.

A small minority of the fathers said that they supported their partners but that the support was not reciprocated. These marriages or partnerships were those in the greatest danger of falling apart, and since the interviews three of these marriages/partnerships have folded.

When the parents were asked to describe their disabled child or children, many mothers began by giving the child's diagnostic label. No father did that. They immediately described the child's charm, personality, ability or talent. Then they often gave an account of what they and the child did together, such as going for drives, walking, attending sports events, playing ball, swimming and such like.

When parental birth leave was extended in 2001, and fathers were given the right to take three months of work to take care of their new baby, things changed for young fathers. All but one of the fathers in the *Citizens* group made use of this opportunity, to their delight. Thor, the father in the third vignette, took his child alone to the SDCC when his wife was ill, and discovered "that fathers were at least as important to the child as mothers". Remember also how, despite his wife's dismay, he handled the transition of his son into preschool, and how pleased he was to be able to put his tools away, grab the pots and pans, care for both his children and get to know them. Subsequently, he reduced his working hours so he could have more time with his family. This and other similar stories in the data indicate that the fathers of the youngest children were learning to participate in family life in a different way from the previous generations. Values were shifting, yet no other group of fathers in this research was under as much pressure to work hard for long hours as were the fathers in the *Citizens* group at the height of the economic boom.

Unlike the mothers, a number of fathers complained that they could no longer partake in old hobbies or sport because of demands due to their disabled child and the family. For some of the fathers such interests also coincided with their work. A father who is a known sportsman and competes regularly in athletics tournaments at home and abroad felt that his wife and family circumstances would eventually force him to give that up, and with it a job he loves. He was part of a dual career family, and his absences put an almost impossible strain on his wife, who tried to keep both her work and family together and provide necessary services for their child, who has a regressive genetic difference. The father's dilemma was made even more excruciating because he was familiar with the genetic difference from his own background: he had a sibling with the same deteriorating impairment. He had grown up with his parents' struggles for support, and he knew that the genetic difference would probably lead his own child into profound deterioration and an early death. Fathers were more likely than the mothers to mention that they needed more time with their partners or wives away from the children.

A minority of fathers expressed frustration at having a disabled child in the family. A few complained that their disabled son or daughter was too difficult to handle. I was even given unasked-for "privileged information", when a father would complain about getting too little attention from his wife, or that she was too tired, preoccupied or unwilling to have sex, and that he was cheating on the wife with another woman. Both partners in one family with three disabled children stated, independently of each other, that their marriage was long since over. They wanted a divorce, but that was not possible, because of their tightly scheduled routine balancing work, childcare and engagement with the disability services.

Finally, most of the fathers (who were generally the main breadwinners in their families) expressed worries or concerns about money and their ability to provide adequately for their family. This is understandable, because even in a country where most special services for disabled children are free or largely free of charge, and subsidies can be found to cover part of any extra cost, having a disabled and sometimes even a sick child or children involves taking time off work. For some it also meant staying in Reykjavík for weeks or even months on end while the child was diagnosed, tested, treated or hospitalised. Back home, meanwhile, the family home, the other children and a livelihood had to be kept going. Cars had to be maintained to operate safely in the Icelandic climate, and petrol costs mounted. As some disabled children's needs changed, homes and their environments had to be made accessible. Grants could be had for some of this work but not all. The general changes in standards of living and public consumption, at least in and around the main urban areas, added pressure on fathers to provide well for their families. This and the human *rights* perspective on formal support to disabled children and their families fuelled both the fathers' economic worries and their discontent. If having a disabled child was a public issue, why was there not more help out there, and why was it so complex to access even when it was available in theory? In the light of all this, the formal support available in the larger experimental communities was treasured by both parents, and access to informal support from bonding and bridging social capital networks made a huge difference to those families where that was at all available.

We have seen that fathers appreciated what formal supports were available and supported their wives in trying to obtain services. Mostly they let their wives deal with family and friends, and kept on the sidelines. Changes in social policy affected, and in many ways improved, the quality of life of many of these families, but from the fathers' point of view the most significant changes were related to the new and important paternity leave, which was available only to the *Citizens*. Surprisingly many fathers got little or no personal support, either from their informal networks or from the disability service apparatus, and depended on their wives for personal emotional support. The social roles of the fathers and husbands were "viscosious" in the sense that they tried to level the family playing-field and fill the gaps stemming from their family lives with a difference. They did this by taking on tasks that their wives could not or would not deal with. This caused many fathers considerable stress and conflict, as they tried to juggle the demands of work, family, personal interests, their own emotions, and the difficulties of dealing with the various disability, educational and health services. Their wives were on the whole the skippers on the family boat, but the fathers represented the crew.

Chapter 7

ORDINARY LIVES WITH A DIFFERENCE: SOCIAL CAPITAL, POWER GAMES AND PARENTAL REACTIONS

Up to this point, this book has focused on the struggles and dilemmas of family life as social policy and society evolved and impacted the parents and their family lives. However, the data reveal much more. A life with a disabled child or children is by no means all doom, gloom and struggle, and almost all the families fall eventually into what they see as "an ordinary life with a difference". There are many stories of happy moments, of close and loving relationships between couples, of everyday disputes like who should take out the rubbish or do the washing up. And there are stories of family gatherings, laughter, outings with the children, holidays with and without the children, and of the talents and activities of the non-disabled children in the families. In short these are stories of "ordinary lives with a difference" (see also Ferguson, 2001). Some of these stories are filled with humour, like the story told by a mother about a distant paternal aunt who came on a visit and mistook the disabled child for his non-disabled sibling, took him for a walk, and came back beaming, saying to the mother "at least this one is OK, fantastically bright". The child (who had autism) had repeated as best he could every single sentence his aunt spoke to him on their walk. Many other writers have mentioned such stories. Sometimes events around the home and the disabled child get so out of kilter that, at least in retrospect, it seems hilarious. This is also common in parents' writing. The Fergusons, for example (2001), use humour in their article *Winks, blinks, squints and twitches: Looking for disability, culture and self-determination through our son's left eye*, where they describe a chain of dismal events in their home the day the canary died. Then they go on to analyse and discuss the cultural meaning of disability, disabled adulthood and other academic issues. Further, several parents of disabled children tell of delightful mistakes, mistaken identities and odd happenings in their encounters with the ordinary world (Bérubé, 1996; Bjarnason, 2003; Rix, 2003; Schaefer, 1982). These tales often highlight how the so-called ordinary events of life get turned on their head and become surrealistic, stupid or odd, because outsiders do not take account of the child's difference or the parents' ordinary reactions to extraordinary circumstances.

The stresses and dilemmas in the family occur primarily around the birth and the diagnosis of a disabled child. But they may also arise at every transition in the child's life, or when changes occur in the family, destabilising its ideologies (Sætersdal, 1997), activity settings, rhythms and routines (see Bjarnason, 2004, pp. 136-138). Any change can upset the delicate balance of family arrangements; it might involve father or mother changing their job or work hours, a new child being born, big sister getting married, Christmas, summer or Easter holidays. Changes in services at the school or preschool, the physiotherapy routine, the provisions of the respite services, a teachers' strike, teachers attending training courses, changes in the personal life of a family member or helper, can also upset this balance and affect the lives of all family members. In such situations everyone in the family may be called upon to reschedule their plans, and many of the mothers involved in this study were masters at inventing plans B and C and D. Sometimes the older siblings were relied upon for help, but many parents were reluctant to put too much responsibility on their other children. A mother of four children in the *Settlers* group explained: "They are entitled to their own lives and friends. I try and protect them. It is hard enough for them at home, where so much of my attention is inevitably on our Ásgeir". This statement also captures the concerns of many parents about possibly neglecting their other children, putting too much responsibility on their shoulders, not paying enough attention to their feelings, achievements or well-being. A few parents said they had suggested that their other children should attend a siblings' workshop, enabling them to talk to other children in similar circumstances. Some had done so, some found it useful, others not. But despite the parents' worries and concerns over protecting their other children, the siblings were most often described as loving, protective of their disabled sibling, unusually mature, considerate and able. Ordinary sibling rivalry obviously occurred, but also fun, games and inclusion with the siblings' circle of friends. In eight out of the seventy-five families, however, the parents mentioned that one or more of their older children (mostly older boys) had ended up with "the wrong crowd" and got involved in drugs, drink and/or crime. These parents blamed that on themselves and how they might have neglected these children.

LONELINESS

Adapting to changes in family rhythms and routines is much easier if you have a number of people in your close network to call upon for help. Surprisingly few parents in this study had that luxury in their everyday lives. A theme common to all the parent narratives is loneliness. Both parents told of feeling acute emotional loneliness at the times of suspected impairment, in the years immediately after diagnosis, at times of transition, and when they felt the need to fight for services and supports for their child and family. Ragna in the *Pioneer* group, the mother of Helga born with a physical impairment, said:

> My husband is a tower of strength, always has been. We have gone through good times and troubled times, always together. We have loved each other since we first met. I was only fifteen and he nineteen… All our children are doing really well, Helga is fine. She is an adult now. She has a part time job she likes, shares a home with a friend, gets much of the help she needs… and leads as normal a life as possible with her difficulties. I should be grateful and relieved, and I am. Yet, I often wake up in the night, especially if something is about to change. I feel empty and scared; I cry and am utterly sorry for myself. I have done this, ever since she was a baby… [On these occasions] I feel so totally alone. My husband may be sleeping right next to me, but I don't want to wake him, and even if I did, I don't think I could reach him,…he would not understand…

And a father from the *Settlers* group said:

> When I despair and feel that I do not know how to deal with all the things she wants me to…, I cannot talk to her then…, I go for long walks, or do things around the house. I have been on many long walks…

The loneliness hits hardest at the time of the birth, if the impairment was immediately detectable, or in the anticipatory period leading up to diagnosis (see Booth, 1978). It was the time when many of the mothers especially felt the fathers to be in denial, and that neither friends, family, nor the professionals heard their concerns, or if they were heard, they were not taken seriously (see also Bjarnason, 2004). This period could last from a few days to a few years, depending upon how long it took to get the diagnosis. At the diagnosis, most of the parents interviewed experienced acute anomie, affecting their own sense of identity, their self-image, their fundamental trust in themselves and each other as parents and partners. This could also erode particularly the wives' trust in their spouses, and in other close family members and best friends. The type and availability of formal and informal support played a key role in shortening or extending this period of anomie, and in the reconstruction of identities.

ENGAGING WITH SOCIAL CAPITAL

Where the informal network remained strong and access to the flow of bonding, bridging and linking capital was open and available, where the parents felt listened to and not disempowered, and where waiting lists were short or non-existent, parents had an easier time reinventing their families with a difference than when these things were lacking.

Engaging With Bonding Social Capital

Contrary to what might be thought to be the case in a small face-to-face society like Iceland, a majority of the parents in all the groups reported that they lost contact with members of their families, at least for a time. Family members, including mothers and mothers-in-law, were felt to show too much or too little concern for the couple and the disabled infant; to help too much, in the wrong way or not at all; or they said something or made a gesture that hurt, or added to the couple's problems by feeling too sorry for them. Such relatives became unwelcome.

Similar things happened with friends. Old friends disappeared, drifted away or did or said something hurtful, and were discarded. That frequently happened when people were for some reason tactless, or avoided the parents and their disabled child out of shyness and uncertainty. Trust between people who had formerly been close would be lost for no apparent reason, and was hard to re-establish. Such an experience could leave deep wounds, even as time passed and the families adjusted to their new situation. Many, especially the mothers, said that they had expected help from their nearest and dearest, but found, to their dismay, that the informal network was less supportive than anticipated. A mother from the *Explorers* group, with a child with CP said:

> It was a very dark winter. We were alone…. You would have thought that your nearest family and friends would rally around you and the baby that needed so much. But nobody came except my mother…and that was not so good because she felt so sorry for us and wanted to take charge…

This woman, like many other parents, found that people in her closest network drifted away when the strain on bonding capital proved too great. A mother from the *Citizens* group, who had a disabled child in 2003, told this story;

> About a month after Aron was born, my best (girl) friend called and said: "Darling, have you got over it yet?" My world collapsed. I never want to see her or speak to her again.

Several couples explained the loss of contact with former friends as being caused by the demands on their time – too taxing for extra-curricular activities. I had anticipated that this might be the case for families in the *Settlers* and the *Citizens* groups, particularly those who lived in urban sectors, but less so for the older parents, and for parents in rural areas where life went on at a slower pace. But I was wrong. There is strong evidence in the data that bonding social capital typically weakened on diagnosis of a disabled child in the family, in all the groups, and in both urban and rural communities. While drawing on such bonding social capital as remained available, parents had to rely mostly on each other and their other children. The importance of those who stayed and stood by the family was highly valued. Dögg, a mother of two children born in the late 1970s and early 1980s with a genetic difference that would eventually lead to their early deaths, said:

> I was hurt and alone. I thought everybody would want to help, but that did not happen. When our second child was born with the same problem, some of our friends and family did not even ask how we were getting along or how they were doing… These were dark days. What saved us was my mother who called every day, my girlfriend, Anna…and the wonderful doctor who has never let us down.

Other, but fewer, families experienced both practical and emotional help and understanding from their nearest and dearest. Thor and Helga in the third vignette experienced that their extended families, their friends and their community stood by them. Such support made all the difference to that family.

Informal support was mostly given by the child's grandmothers (mostly the maternal grandmother), a grandfather, and the mothers' sisters or sisters-in-law. The woman's friends are seldom described as giving practical help such as babysitting or helping with housework. Still, most of the mothers had at least one girlfriend with whom they could talk. Such girlfriends lent a listening ear, provided suggestions or a shoulder to lean on.

As we have seen in Chapter 6, fathers seldom experienced such personal support except from their wives, or occasionally from one or both of their parents or a sibling. A father from the *Explorers* group, whose son, labelled with autism, was still living at home in 2006, said:

> We could not really go anywhere together when he was little. We still do not. If she was out or at a meeting I looked after the kids... Even when her parents took the kids, we were too tired to go anywhere. My folks have always been useless ...[at helping us] and my mother is still scared of Siggi, and cannot handle him. They do not understand. My wife feels that they judge us for not keeping him in line. Her parents are younger and we trust them... We do not discuss this with our friends. They have enough to deal with in their own lives. We have drifted apart. This is our problem, always was... We will keep Siggi at home as long as we can. [My wife] does not want him in a group home. We do what we can and hope for the best...

There is also evidence in the data that new bonding capital got built at a time when access to the former trusted network had weakened. Sylvía told this story:

> At first I felt totally abandoned by my [extended] family. Even my mother could not accept the birth of Tomas at first. They stayed away, but a woman I hardly new, a neighbour much older than me, suddenly stepped in. She is the wife of my husband's colleague. Before [the birth of Tomas] we had barely exchanged greetings. All of a sudden she appeared on our doorstep... She never offered to help, she just came and did what had to be done. She would make some coffee, chat, take care of the washing or look after the children while I took a nap. She did all this in such a way that I hardly noticed at the time. I don't know what I would have done without her. She is still one of my best friends... Later, she even introduced me to her girlfriends who included me in their group.

Fifteen years on she is a valued member of that circle of women friends, ten to twenty years older than herself. Most are either teachers or artists and they have known each other since their youth. They meet regularly, help each other out and enjoy each other's company. Sylvía's bonding capital has extended much further than she would have thought possible.

Engaging with Bridging and Linking Social Capital

Many, but by no means all, the parents reported that in times of crisis they had been able to pick up the phone, send an email or meet with friendly professionals, administrators, politicians, MPs and even a government minister in search for help. This is common practice in a small face-to-face society like Iceland, but certainly not unknown in larger societies. Access to and engagement with bridging and linking social capital is connected with people's social status, background and social situations. The data show clearly that access to and engagement with bridging and linking social capital was likely to empower the parents and make them more able to access formal support and thus fulfil their and their disabled child's needs as they understood them. As we have seen, the mothers were most likely to engage with bridging capital; for example working with professionals such as doctors, teachers and therapists on a regular basis, and attending local parents' groups. In cases where mutual trust and understanding developed between those mothers/parents and the professionals, it could open up a well of information and access to resources the family did otherwise not have or even know about. Several of these people were very supportive to the disabled child and his or her mothers/parents, but a prerequisite for such mutual trust was too often based on whether or not the mothers/parents bought into the professional ideology (often medical model ideology). Mutual trust tended to be based on the mothers/parents buying into the ideology and procedures of the particular professionals, learning their jargon and accepting their approaches and solutions. The evidence suggests that when that did not follow suit, the parents felt disrespected or not listened to by the professionals. That eroded trust, could be a recipe for conflict, or dissolution of the parents. Such parents sometimes felt that they were labelled "difficult parents" and that this in itself diminished their access and possible engagement with professional bridging capital.

Fathers, more than the mothers, had access to linking social capital; to persons or groups in very different power and status positions to themselves who were possibly able to help when conflicts occurred between the family and the system. The fathers were more likely than the mothers to belong to political parties or professional associations, have contact with relatives in important bureaucratic occupations. Both parents could at times rake up contacts with old schoolmates, but especially if they themselves had upper-secondary school or university education. A number of the fathers in this study also belonged to male-dominated leisure groups such as the Masons, Lions or Odd fellows, attended largely by men from the middle and upper social strata. In a few cases, the fathers admitted that they had access to individuals with significant social influence via the AA movement. One father said that he had been able to pull some strings for his disabled child at the Ministry of Social Affairs, by "asking his golf-buddy for advice". A few parents, like Grímur, became community leaders or advocates in the affairs of disabled people. That helped build both bridging and linking capital. Despite the fact that many of those parents admitted that they were shy to make use of such contacts on behalf of their own child and family, some had either done so at least once, or were prepared to pull such strings in cases of emergency. Access to and engagement with bridging and linking capital is of vital importance to all these parents and their children, but they are unevenly distributed.

Power Games and Gate-Keepers

As the medicalization of difference continues and gradually more groups of disability labels appear, getting the "right" label for the child's difference is the key to all formal support. Accessing that label and support, however, could turn into a nightmare, as the second vignette illustrates. The power games reported were many and excruciating for the parents involved. Parents of children eventually diagnosed on the autistic spectrum were amongst the parents hardest hit by these games, as were some parents who did not want to follow some particular professional advice. Professionals can, and frequently do, act as gate-keepers (Bjarnason, 2009a; Lundeby and Tøssebro, 2008b). Doctors and the SDCC wield the power to define the child's and the family's problems and needs, and can help or hinder the family in accessing formal support. According to Foucault, power and the exercise of power in itself is neither good nor bad, but productive or repressive, and it produces subjects and spaces. Certain people, including doctors, psychologists, educators and others, channel the power of institutions. The doctors display knowledge and exercise power through their *medical gaze* (Foucault, 1963/1975) channelled to them as individuals through the institutions of medicine. For parents seeking treatment, diagnosis, or access to services and grants, the doctor's power was vital, whether or not they agreed with the doctor's verdict. Thus, parents were unable to oppose the doctor's or the SDCC's diagnosis, or having their children transformed into "socially constructed diagnosed subjects" and even placed within "special spaces" (Jóhannesson, 2006). Teachers, principals in preschools and schools, rehabilitation therapists and even bureaucrats can be seen to display knowledge and exercise power in a similar, but somewhat less firm manner, for productive or repressive purposes.

When repressive power was at play, professionals signified gate-keepers from the parents' perspective. In the second vignette, it emerges that the harder Mary pushed for diagnosis and services, the more obstacles were put in her and her family's way. This is another theme running through the data, in particular when the child's diagnosis turned out to be complex, or if the parents wanted specific special services, or generic services with special support added on (such as ordinary schooling) that did not fit the bureaucratic forms and constructed spaces. Waiting lists, formal rules, informal rules and practices of organisations were used as excuses for not complying with the parents' wishes. Even unskilled or semi-skilled staff could place themselves in the gate-keeper's role. Mary and Peter, for example, used to take turns to drive their daughter Kristín for physiotherapy first thing each day, as a result of which she would arrive at her preschool too late for the regular breakfast hour; the preschool staff refused to bend the routine and serve her some yoghurt, so Mary or Peter had to stay and feed her, and would therefore be late for work.

Gate-keepers were almost invariably used to try and force the parents in line when they were thought to overstep their boundaries. Headmasters or teachers in schools where a particular child was not welcome manipulated the parents by telling them how many "normal" children with learning problems could be helped for the money "their child" would cost the school, the community and the taxpayer. Some parents withdrew their applications as a consequence, while others stubbornly refused to do so, often earning more gate-keeping in response. The arguments put forward were: the school did not have the same expertise as a different school; it would be harmful to the child not to make use of that other school's expertise; the child would not find friends at this school; they lacked equipment, and so forth. The data are littered with such examples. The only difference in the parent narratives on this subject over time is how some of the gate-keepers appear gradually more careful and diplomatic in how they express their objections.

PARENTAL REACTIONS

Many parents learnt how to deal with the gate-keepers. In the cruel dance of these power games, some parents became experts at anticipating obstacles and side-stepping them, often inventing new ways of serving their disabled child. These were the strong, active parents in each of the groups. Strong, active parents were not necessarily financially better off than the rest. These were parents who could access and engage with a broad base of social capital and who made full use of it when needed to secure the outcomes they envisaged. Many of these solutions eventually rippled through systems or organisations and became accepted standard practice, the new rule or legal clause. Other parents, equally strong but less assertive, often with less access to linking and bridging capital, and less optimistic about their ability to affect change, would react and lobby for their child's *right*, when they felt that a law or a formal regulation had been broken. A third way of responding to hindrances and gate-keeping was simply to wait one's turn, retreat, feel passive or hopeless, and accept such support as was delivered, even when they felt it did not match their or their child's needs. Some, but not all, of these parents were amongst the least educated and the least financially well-off parents in the study.

This can be summarised as follows:

-Strong optimistic partnerships. Open access to bridging and linking social capital; coincides with pro-active parental responses, and a belief in own capacity to affect change.

- Strong but pessimistic/"realistic" partnerships. Moderate access to bridging and linking social capital; coincides with re-active parental responses, and a strong belief in the system's/ professionals' duty to provide required services. A moderate belief in own capacity to affect change.

- Weak partnerships. Little access to social capital; coincides with passive acceptance of services on offer, or hopelessness/anomie vis-à-vis service systems and professionals.

These parental responses go across the data. They appear to be situated partly in the nature and mutuality of the couples' relationships, and in their access to and engagement with social capital. Single parents were found in all three categories. Accessing the flow of bridging and linking capital is related to social status, education, place, political party membership and family connections. The parents who drove the changes in social policy were parents who fit the first category: the strong and active parents in all four groups. They may not all have been well educated, formally speaking, and certainly not all upper or middle class, but they were all positive in their attitude to their own ability to affect change, supportive of each other, and able to generalise from their experiences about the predicaments of other families. All had access to a broad-based bridging and linking social capital or were able to build social capital around themselves and others.

The strong, pessimistic, or as some described themselves, "realistic" couples, "kept to themselves", "dealt with their own", "made the best of what they had", "were unwilling to push" or "to jump the queue". They were more willing to trust the systems or the professionals, and more likely to confess their own lack of skills in the various professionals' areas. Many of these parents were average to well educated, and almost all described themselves as "private people". Even though they might have access to bridging and linking social capital, most were reluctant to use that for the purpose of getting favours for themselves or their families, unless they felt that a law or a formal rule, a *right*, had been broken.

The weak parents were those whose mutuality as couples was less self-evident than in the other pair relations. For some the relationship itself seemed weak, at other times one of the spouses, mostly the father, was absent for extended periods. One parent (usually the mother, but in two cases the father) dealt with all family issues including issues related to the child's disability and the service system. The fathers were the main breadwinners, often working very long hours. One father was in prison. These families had for the most part little access to any form of social capital. Most of the mothers accepted gratefully what formal support was on offer, even if they were concerned about particular aspects of the service.

A number of the mothers in this category were exhausted, experienced burnout, had health problems or had lost trust in the professionals after trying to fight losing battles with the SSI, the schools or the disability services. Parents who are, for whatever reason, disempowered are likely to turn into weak parents, unable to protect themselves and their children from the repressive elements of professional power and the gaze (Foucault, 1963/1975).

Access to social capital can buffer that kind of repression. For all the families, the importance of engaging with social capital is one of the clearest lessons from the study. It impacts relationships at all levels, micro, mezzo and macro, and explains the families' aptitudes to solicit necessary and sufficient support for their disabled child and for other similarly situated families. It affects their ability to innovate or implement changes in the formal support systems, submit to what support is on offer, or give up the struggle. Financial resources alone do not secure such support except perhaps for the few very rich. Support needs to be aimed at the family as a unit, not just the disabled child or children. For that to happen, social capital needs to be built, nurtured, and accessible in time of need.

CONCLUSION

The purpose of this book is to make a contribution to our understanding of parents of disabled children in a changing ideological and social policy climate. The small size of the Icelandic society enables me to look over changes impacting parents' experiences over a period of time, and to cover changes in social policy aimed at supporting families with disabled children, as it evolved from no such support to significant but mismatched support in an entire social system. The study set out to describe and explore the experience of parents of disabled children and young people of giving birth to and bringing up a disabled child – and their experience of different formal and informal support for the child and the family. By using the ideas of private troubles and public issues (Berger 1963) the study compares the experiences of parents of disabled children born over a 33-year period (1974-2007), a period of significant changes in law and services aimed at families and disabled children. I found that there is a gradual shift of emphasis away from disability in the family being simply a private trouble towards it becoming also a public issue, transferring the responsibility for supporting a disabled child on to the state, local municipalities and society at large and based on claims to the child's *right* as a citizen. I have also explored whether and in what way there is a connection between the support available and the decisions and choices that parents make on their disabled children's behalf, e.g. regarding their placement in segregated or inclusive settings, and even, in the late 1990s, with almost universal prenatal scanning of pregnant women, whether or not a foetus identified with a difference should be born. The findings here present a mixed picture; the evidence suggests, however, that education, community membership and home municipality play a part in parents' choices, but also their access to and engagement with bonding, bridging and linking capital. Finally I set out to explore the positive and negative implications of increased specialization and expansion of formal services directed towards disabled children and their families on their full and active participation in society, and identify in what way specialized and generic support can empower disabled children and their families. The evidence is clear that, overall, the lives of disabled children and their families have improved greatly over the period of time in question. Disabled people including children have become more visible in our schools and society. Economic growth, increased standard of living and changes in ideology towards inclusion play a part in explaining that, but the expansion of specialised and generic formal services and the increase of available specialists also play a part. However, the selfsame formal support structure has become difficult to access, complex, fragmented and unclear. Medicine has certainly advanced but somehow the social incompetence of some medical doctors and staff reflected in the parents' narratives is seriously problematic and hurtful. However, the data also showed that some individuals within the health system showed extraordinary care and concern in supporting a few of the parents and their children. Medical doctors' privilege to diagnose and eventually dole out more and more labels to children that do not fit the norm is problematic. On the one hand such labels are seen to be tickets to special additional support for these children and their families. On the other hand they may result in constructing the disabled children as *social artifacts*, to be dealt with as residual categories, different from other children. That may disempower disabled children and their families; push them to the edge of the schools and estrange them from mainstream schools and society. Parents continue to struggle for their disabled child's or children's support, education and other rights, but for what, how and why has changed. Parents' expectations of what ordinary life entails have changed.

The overall findings demonstrate parents' struggles and capacities and amazing resilience as they go on with their ordinary lives. These findings are impressive, yet they coincide with the findings of other researchers in several other western type countries (see Ferguson, 2001a; Goodley, 2007; Goodley and Lawthom, 2008; McLaughlin, Goodley, Clavering, and Fisher, 2008; Lundeby and Tøssebro, 2008b; Sætersdal, 1997). Apart from idiosyncratic differences in such research findings due to differences in welfare state systems and cultures, the plight of parents of disabled children is similar in what we have come to think of as the western world. However one thing sticks out in the Icelandic findings which makes them differ from much other parent research I am aware of. Whereas poverty and housing problems appear common amongst lower class families with disabled children in Britain and the USA (see McLaughlin, Goodley, Clavering, and Fisher, 2008) and to a lesser extent (mitigated by the welfare systems) in Scandinavia (Tøssebro and Lundeby, 2002; Lundeby and Tøssebro, 2008a, 2008b), this was not the case in the Icelandic study. Only two families in this research can be described as suffering from acute economic hardship and being totally dependent on social assistance for their livelihood. The explanation for this may primarily to be found in the overall Icelandic economic growth from the 1970s up to 2008, the near full employment of its labour force and high percentage of women's economic participation, rather than in the efficiency and generosity of the specific disability policy and benefit schemes of the state and its municipalities. It is for example noteworthy that most of the mothers interviewed for this study were partially or fully employed at the time of the interviews despite caring for their disabled child or children within their families. The fact that the Icelandic findings bear a family resemblance to similar findings elsewhere, hopefully adds to their trustworthiness and transferability, and will make them useful to researchers and policy makers beyond Iceland.

The study has used the issue of private troubles and public issues in order to capture the shift in how the different groups of parents express the locus of responsibilities for disability in their families. The oldest parents accepted their plight as their private trouble to be dealt with within their families, but gradually the subsequent parents' groups claimed that their disabled child or children were also the responsibility of the state, the community and society at large. The youngest parent group (which I have labelled the *Citizens of the welfare state*) demonstrate clearly that they expect the state and their communities to provide the necessary formal support to their disabled child and family, on the grounds of what they see as their disabled child's *human right*. This raises the question whether defining disability as a public issue may lead to an evasion of responsibility: could that lead to the perception that disability is everyone's responsibility and yet no-one's responsibility? If so, might that in practice result in an overall erosion of responsibilities for providing appropriate services and support, both formal and informal, to such children and their families? This could become an issue for concern. The Icelandic government needs to make substantial cuts to its welfare and other public spending in order to avoid national bankruptcy, and to repay the enormous foreign debt accumulated by unscrupulous bankers and businessmen during the economic bubble leading to the economic collapse; the hardest hit by such cuts are likely to be the most vulnerable groups in the country – the old, the unemployed, schoolchildren, the sick, and disabled people and their families. If the responsibility for supporting vulnerable people is thus eroded, there is a danger of anomie spreading within society. That invites neglect and hardship for those with the least private resources. In such a climate it is of utmost importance to be on guard, and to strengthen human rights and children's rights with all possible means. These are urgent and current issues for the present government, the legislature and the general public, as they attempt to re-establish the Icelandic economy and society.

APPENDIX 1

Year	Education: The Educational System	Health: General Health Services	Social Services: General Public Welfare	Social Services: Disability Issues and Law	Social Services: Regional Services
1900s - 1950s	1907: First compulsory school act appeared 1911: University of Iceland established	1902: First hospital opened 1930: First state-owned hospital opened. 1932: Country divided into health regions	1936: Beginning of a National Social Insurance Administration 1946: Ministry of Social Affairs established. 1947: Social Insurance further developed with Act nr. 80/1947.	1924: Daycare for disadvantaged children 1930: First institution for people with intellectual impairment.	
1960s	1960's: No schooling for disabled students except students with hearing or sight difficulties – and some schooling institutions	1969: Ministry of Health and Social Security established to take over health services and the pension and benefit system		1950s and 1960s: Institutions for disabled people established. 1965: Kjarvalshús Assessment Centre for children established.	

1970s	1961: Special school for students with IQ 50-75 1969: A boarding school opened for children with physical disabilities.			
	1973: Administration of preschools moved to the Ministry of Education. 1974: New school act. All children to complete schooling. School chosen depended on IQ 1974: First modern school for students with IQ 50-75. 1977: Statutory regulation on special education	1975: Ultrasound introduced.	1970: New legal act passed on public insurance. The SSI administers Pension Insurance, Health Insurance and Occupational Injury Insurance. Unemployment benefits are administered by the Department for Labour, Family benefits by the directorate of Internal Revenue	1979: Law on Assistance to the "Mentally Retarded" marked beginning of community support services for persons with disability	1979: Area Boards for services for people with mental retardation.
1980s	1980: First school for students with IQ below 50.	1986: A State Diagnostic Centre opened	1986: A centre for the provision of mechanical aids such as wheelchairs for disabled people was established under the SSI	1983: Law on Assistance to people with mental disabilities broadened to reach also people with physical and sensory impairment	1983: Area Boards for the services of disabled people.

1990s	1988: New act declares Upper secondary schools are for everyone 1990's: All preschool children were in regular preschools 1991: Act on the transference of services from state to local municipalities. 1994: Salamanca Declaration signed making inclusive education the policy for all school levels apart from university level. 1994: Preschools legally defined as the first school level. 1996: Compulsory school administration moved to municipalities. 1996: Upper-secondary schools required by law to provide special classes 1998: Statutory Regulation on special education.	1986: All pregnant women in Iceland offered free ultrasound in the 18th or 19th week. 1990s: Reykjavik-based hospitals amalgamated into the "National University Hospital".	1994: Act on Experimental Municipalities passed	1986: A State Diagnostic Centre opened 1990's: Most institutions and special schools for disabled people closed down. 1992: Act On the Affairs of the Disabled (based on the Law on Assistance to the Mentally Retarded). Changes in the legislation gradually brought more special services; group homes, sheltered workshops, day centres, and later supported flats and supported work in the regular job market.	1991: Act on the transference of services from state to local municipalities – did not apply to services under the Disability Legislation 1994: Act on Experimental Municipalities passed; two municipalities experiment with joining or co-ordinating services for disabled people and their families. Three more did the same – results felt to be

				successful, more flexible and individualised to each child's and family's needs.
2000s	Emphasis on inclusive placement and practices. Parents of disabled students can choose special or regular school. 2001: Reykjavik municipality policy to develop inclusive education further. 2001: Students with disabilities have option of 4-year Upper Secondary schooling instead of only 2 years. 2001: The Deaf School closed, deaf students in regular school. 2001: Most students with special needs served in regular compulsory schools. All students served in		2001: Parental birth benefits 9 months: 3 months for each parent and 3 months for both together. Administered first by SSI and with a new Act 2008 administered by the Department of Labour 2007: All social security matters apart from those directly concerned with health moved to the Ministry of Social Affairs and Social Security. 2008: Administration of the SSI and social security moved to the Ministry of Social Affairs and Social Security.	2003: legislation on the State Diagnostic and Counselling Centre (the law 83/2003) 2009: plan to move the administration of the affairs of disabled people over to municipalities by 2011.

regular preschools. The first "experimental" university program for a few students with intellectual impairment. 2002: A new special school for students with behavioural problems. 2008: New compulsary school act. The words "Inclusive education" appear for the first time in the legal text. Plans to replace the two existing special schools for students with intellectual impairment .			

APPENDIX 2. WALKING ON EGGSHELLS: SOME ETHICAL ISSUES IN RESEARCH WITH PEOPLE IN VULNERABLE SITUATIONS

ABSTRACT

Qualitative inquiry aims at understanding the meaning of human action. It involves a variety of social inquiry which has its roots in hermeneutics, phenomenology and the tradition of Verstehen. It encompasses all forms of social research that involves data in the forms of words and gestures that form the basis for meaning making, and a broad base of methods, techniques and theoretical approaches applied to gather and interpret the data (Schwandt, 2001). This chapter is about some ethical issues at stake when qualitative inquiry involves people in vulnerable situations such as the young, the very old, the sick or disabled or minority groups of people often labelled as "the other". Some such inquiry is done in partnership with the subjects involved with the aim of empowering the subjects and work towards improving the quality of their lives (Oliver, 1990, Barnes, Mercer, and Shakespeare, 1999). Other such inquiry is carried out by disability researchers and other social scientists without the participation of the subjects in the research process (Shakespeare, 2006, Vehmas, 2008). Ethical issues and dilemmas appear at every juncture of the research process and also when the researcher decides what to publish and why.

The chapter starts with some of the issues and experiences the author brings to the table after working in the field of inclusive education and disability research for over three decades. Next it offers some notes on qualitative inquiry and then it moves on to explore ethics, ethical issues and dilemmas inevitably part and parcel of all such inquiry. Then it applies examples from the author's fieldwork to the discussion of ethical issues and dilemmas encountered in qualitative research with people in vulnerable situations. Examples are in particular drawn from the author's recent study that involved interviews with Icelandic parents of disabled children; the children were born over a period of 35 years (1974-2007) in a time of significant socio-political change in both Icelandic disability- and social policy and society.

The ethical issues and dilemmas touched upon include those related to gaining access, the interview situation itself including the building of rapport and the fine line between gathering the data, data analysis, ethical issues related to what to select from privileged knowledge (a concept given me by Dianne Ferguson 2009), if anything, and other concerns with the writing up of sensitive data analysis. Finally, some thought is given to publications, their interpretations by the reader and their use or abuse.

INTRODUCTION

The chapter explores some of the many ethical problems that are likely to confront qualitative researchers studying people in vulnerable situations within the field of disability studies and special and inclusive educational research. Examples are taken from my own research, experiences gathered over the last 30 years in the field, but particularly from my current research into how parents of disabled children view their lives and the formal and informal supports made available to them over time. The examples include moral and ethical challenges, dilemmas and pitfalls one is likely to encounter as a researcher studying people in vulnerable situations in a small society where face to face interaction characterizes social encounters, or in local communities of larger societies, where people know or know of each other.

The chapter starts with some of the issues and experiences I bring to the table from my own work experiences. Next it offers some notes on qualitative inquiry. Then it moves on to explore ethics, and some ethical issues and dilemmas encountered in the context of qualitative inquiry. Then it applies examples from my own fieldwork, particularly the gathering of data through interviews, to the discussion of ethical issues and dilemmas encountered in qualitative research with people in vulnerable situations. The examples are in particular drawn from my recent study that involved interviewing Icelandic parents of disabled children (born 1974-2007) in a time of significant socio-political change in both Icelandic disability- and social policy and society.

The ethical issues and dilemmas touched upon include gaining access, the interview situation itself including the building of rapport, and the ethical challenges found in the interview situation itself. Furthermore, ethical issues related to the data analysis will be discussed, and what to select from *privileged knowledge* (a concept given me by Dianne Ferguson 2009), if anything. The term *privileged knowledge* refers to the kind of things that the person being interviewed tells the interviewer, sometimes deeply private and personal matters they feel the need to share, which may not further the research. Finally the chapter will briefly touch upon other ethical concerns in the writing up of sensitive data and its publication.

BACKGROUND: WHAT DO I BRING TO THE TABLE?

In my work as a qualitative researcher I have often used interviews to gather significant parts of my data combined with observations, participant observations and document analysis. I have interviewed teenagers and their parents, entrepreneurs, bureaucrats, government ministers, fishermen, teachers of all kinds, student teachers, health workers and therapeutic professionals, disabled youth, and family members of disabled children and young people.

Over the past 25 years I have researched issues related to disability and inclusion and exclusion in schools and society (for example Bjarnason, 2002, 2003, 2004, 2009). My interests in those areas are fuelled by my concern with questions about inequality, marginalization and exclusion in modern schools and societies, and by a personal history of becoming a parent in 1980 to a son with significant impairment and an impressive string of labels (Bjarnason, 2003).

In my work I have often been amazed, humbled and even embarrassed by the intimate details people have been willing to share in semi-structured interview situations. Through successes, mistakes and failure I have become keenly aware of how delicate, but also deeply informative and rewarding, research with people in vulnerable situations can be. This chapter shares some of my reflections and lessons learnt in the field.

NOTES ON QUALITATIVE INQUIRY

Qualitative inquiry aims at understanding the meaning of human action. It involves a variety of social inquiry which has its roots in hermeneutics, phenomenology and the tradition of *Verstehen*. It encompasses all forms of social research that involves data in the forms of words and gestures that form the basis for meaning making, and a broad base of methods, techniques and theoretical approaches applied to gather and interpret such data. Thus it may include ethnography, case studies, naturalistic inquiry, ethnography, life histories and narrative inquiry (Schwandt, 2001). When qualitative inquiry involves people in vulnerable situations, it can be a way of giving the subjects a voice in matters concerning their own lives, furthering the understanding of difference, inclusion and exclusion in our schools and society and informing policy makers, professionals and the general public on matters involving diversity, social justice and lived experiences of people labelled as "the Other". In that sense there is a political aspect to such inquiry. Some such inquiry is done in partnership with the subjects involved, where the researcher is seen to be a facilitator, a critic, an advocate or a change agent, counteracting the disempowering dominant groups or structures in society. This is both a political approach aimed at empowering the research subject and those similarly situated, and a way of framing human relations in the research. Other such inquiry is carried out where the researcher is a marginal participant and the researched are seen to be informants for the research purposes. A bitter controversy about these two approaches has recently resulted in a fierce and somewhat ugly debate within the field of disability studies (Shakespeare, 2006, Vehmas, 2008, Dands 2007). On the one hand are those who want to stick with the British social model for its emancipator and political approach, respecting the slogan of British disability advocates "Nothing about us without us" (see O'Brien, 2000, Charlton, 1998), (Oliver,1990, 1996, 2007). On the other hand are those researchers in disability studies, like Tom Shakespeare, who want to be free from the dominant political implications of the British social model approach, favouring what they argue as a more academic pursuit of knowledge. The argument put forward is that the epistemological approach to a research, not the subject matter, should determine the appropriateness and usefulness of the researched as co-researchers (Shakespeare, 2006, Vehmas, 2008).

Most qualitative inquiry involves an ongoing relationship between the researcher and the researched. Such a relationship can be fairly detached and formalized, as when data is gathered by an outside (supposedly "objective") expert who makes an a priori formal contract about the procedure and its ethical parameters with the subjects researched. An example of this is the evaluation of an institution such as a school, hospital or university. But more often the relationship is an ongoing one over a period of time, or intense as in semi-structured interviews. In the field the relations between the researcher and the research participant or subject becomes substantial and subjected to changes in agenda, nuances and vested interests. This calls for heightened awareness of ethical dilemmas and possible pitfalls, and for the researcher's vigilant anticipation of these as the fieldwork unravels.

Before I move on to describe and explore some such ethical issues I have encountered in my work, I will briefly explain what I mean by ethics and ethical issues and dilemmas.

ETHICAL ISSUES AND DILEMMAS

Ethics is the branch of philosophy that explores the nature of moral virtue and evaluates human action. It seeks to study human action and morality through a rational, secular outlook that is based in notions of human happiness or well-being. In the widest sense the subject matter of ethics is the justification of human actions, especially as those actions affect others.

There are basically two traditions in modern philosophical ethics regarding how to determine the ethical character of actions; the first is based on the argument that actions have one intrinsic ethical character but acquire their moral status from the consequences that flow from them. The second tradition is based on the argument that actions are inherently right or wrong. The former is called a *teleological* approach to ethics and the other *deontological* approach to ethics. The former is based in the utilitarian thinking of the British philosopher Jeremy Bentham and refined by John Stuart Mill. It claims that the moral character of action depends on the extent to which actions help or hurt people. Actions that produce more benefit than harm are "right", those that do not are "wrong" (White, 1993). This approach can be problematic based on for example who gets to decide what is or is not a benefit or a harm, and whether or not some harm or suffering to the few is justifiable if it brings benefits and pleasure to the many?

The latter tradition, the *deontological* oriented ethics is based on the approach of Kant's universal moral law: that actions have an intrinsic moral value based on duty or what is the right thing to do. From that perspective some actions are inherently good, such as telling the truth or keeping a promise, others bad, no matter how much good may stem from them, for example lying, coercing or manipulating others. This approach is problematic in its inflexibility, and in who gets to determine whether or not an action is deemed right or wrong (White, 1993). Modern ethical theories include *deontological ethics*, *consequentialist ethics* which is based on the idea of an outcome achieving some good state of affairs, and *virtue ethics*, based on the qualities of character necessary to live well (Schwandt, 2001 p. 73).

In layman's terms, I think it is safe to say that ethics involves a set of customary principles and practices embodying some sort of a normative moral code. Acting in an ethical way implies acting out that code in practice. These codes vary somewhat from culture to culture.

An ethical issue or dilemma arises when there's a conflict between two or more parties, here the researcher and the research participant or informant, if the researcher is benefiting at the expense of the research participant. In other words, when the researcher, using his or her power over the research situation and the research participant, uses the research participant as a *means* to his or her own scientific *end*, hurts or harms the research participant, breaks a promise, or otherwise undermines the trust which must be part and parcel of the relationship between researcher and the research participants. An ethical dilemma can also arise when there's a conflict between moral rules or when one is violated.

As I am neither a philosopher nor ethicist, I dare not dive deeper into this particular theoretical jungle, but all of us involved in educational and disability scholarships, working with people in vulnerable situations, need to take a stance on and reflect upon ethical issues in our work. We need to recognize at all times that ethics, epistemology and politics are intrinsically linked in our everyday work.

When the research participants are people in vulnerable situations, we the researchers must be extra vigilant. People in vulnerable situations can be old people, children and youth, people of all ages with special needs, illness or disability labels and their families, people from minority groups and other disempowered people within our communities.

Sometimes we make errors of judgement or actions and face the painful problem of learning from our mistakes. More often we are just not sure whether or not we managed to live up to our ethical standards, and simultaneously stayed with what constitutes legitimate warranted knowledge of social life, our personal experiences, political commitments, and our responsibilities as students of meaning making. Some such errors may do damage to our academic portrayal, but in the case of people in vulnerable situations, such errors can irrevocably harm the lives of our research participants, people often already vulnerable, disempowered and socially excluded. The doing of qualitative research with people in vulnerable situations can at times be captured by the metaphor of walking on eggshells.

CAPTURING MEANING WITHOUT DOING HARM

Most ethical concerns in the literature and practice of qualitative research revolve around issues of harm, consent, deception and privacy (de Laine, 2000, Punch, 1998, Christians, 2000). As stated above, in qualitative research the researcher enters into a relatively close relationship with the research participants, for example in the participant observer or interview situation. Participation is grounded in trust. Bad mistakes may do harm and close the door for further research. But too much concern with the possible pitfalls can reduce the flexibility of the fieldwork situation and reduce the quality of the data to platitudes of little use for analysis.

Ethics issues are thus always present in qualitative research which is filled with unanticipated occurrences, feelings, lies, unexpected revelations, and unequal roles and power balance. In qualitative research the researcher is himself the research instrument. The researcher, with his or her research participant, creates the text of the research material, interviews, observation, field notes and the research reports. The readers engage with the text of the final report and carry out the final interpretations by engaging with the finished document. Their interpretations may be different to the researcher/s own interpretations and may carry unintended consequences, personal, political and economic.

There are different stances regarding ethical issues in qualitative research. Two of those are of particular concern here. They are the *absolutist stance*, which addresses the following four ethical concerns; protections of participants, prevention of deception, protection of privacy and informed consent. Those who adopt this stance argue that social scientists have no right to invade the privacy of others because such invasion may cause harm to research participants. In contrast, the *relativist stance* states that investigators have absolute freedom to study what they see fit, but they should study only those problems that flow from their own experiences. Agenda setting is most often determined by the personal biography of the researcher. Thus the only reasonable ethical standard is one directed by the researcher's conscience. No single ethical standard can be developed because each situation requires a different ethical stance. From this point of view the researcher is advised to build open sharing relationships with his or her research participants and involve them as much as possible in each and every stage of the research process and interpretations (www.sahealthinfo.org/ethics qualitative.htm).

The difference between these two stances is not clear-cut in practice. For example there is no clear-cut distinction between the public and the private in research that aims at understanding disability in the family, school or society, partnership between parents of children with special educational or other needs and professionals, formal and informal support as experienced by families of children and youth with special needs, the building or erosion of individual or group social capital in schools or out of school activities, to mention just a few research areas. Punch, discussing what can be taken as public and what as private, summarizes the kind of questions that are asked in the research literature on ethical standards in qualitative research as follows (Punch,1998 p.169):

> What is public and what is private? When can research be said to be "harming" people? Does the researcher enjoy any immunity from the law when he or she refuses to disclose information? In what way can one institutionalize ethical norms –such as respect, beneficence, and justice (Reiss, 1979) – to ensure accountability and responsibility in the use and control of human subjects? And to what extent do betrayal of trust, deception and invasion of privacy damage field relationships, make the researcher cynical and devious, enrage the "participants" in research, harm the reputation of social scientific research, and lead to malpractice in the wider society?

Obviously there are no simple answers to any of these questions, but I argue that that should not stop us from considering them very seriously at every juncture of our research work, but not so seriously that we intimidate ourselves and our work and render ourselves incapable of taking risks and being flexible in how we apply our trade.

Both feminist (Oakeley, 1979, 1981) and disability studies scholars (Barnes, Mercer, and Shakespeare, 1999) further muddied the water of what can be seen as the ethical dimension in qualitative research by claiming its political nature. Feminist and disability studies research is carried out not only to develop "new knowledge" or open up new perspectives, but also to give voice to groups that are normally not heard or listened to, unmask injustice, oppression, exploitation and exclusion with the stated aim of improving life for oppressed or people in vulnerable situations. Feminist scholars for example emphasize identification, trust, empathy and non-exploitive relationships in all their research (Finch, 1984, Oakeley, 1981). As Punch reminds us:

> Feminist research by women on women implies "a standpoint epistemology" that not only colours the ethical and moral component of research related to power imbalances in a sexist and racist environment, but

also inhibits deception of the research "subjects". Indeed, the gender and ethnic solidarity between researcher and researched welds that relationship into one of co-operation and collaboration that represents a personal commitment and also a contribution to the interests of women in general (e.g. in giving voice to "hidden women," in generating the "emancipatory praxis" , and in seeing the field settings as "sites of resistance"). (ibid. p. 169)

Disability scholars attempt much the same thing in their work. Disabled scholars such as Colin Barnes, Michel Oliver and Tom Shakespeare have contributed much to the field by opening up new research venues and theoretical perspectives, asking new questions, and applying new and emancipating methods of inquiry. Their work is inspired by them being both *insiders* and *outsiders* in the world of disability. The same applies to thoughtful work by scholars who are also parents or siblings of disabled people (Ferguson, D.L. and Ferguson, P.M, 1993, 1995, Ferguson, P.M. 2001, Turnbull, A and Turnbull, R., Skrtic, 1995).

EXAMPLES FROM THE FIELD

My current research project focuses primarily on four groups of parents of disabled children (born 1974-2007), in all 75 families of one or more children diagnosed with significant impairments, and their experiences of formal supports (by the welfare state including health, education, disability – and social services) and informal supports given by members of the family social networks. The database is 135 semi-structured open-ended interviews with one or both parents, and with 5 couples who selected to abort a foetus with a difference (10 interviews), and 12 interviews with professionals. I also used 3 focus group interviews with staff and professionals and document analysis. I will use examples from that research here to illustrate some of the ethical dilemmas I encountered. These involve selecting the sample, the interviewing process, the data analysis and in reporting the findings.

The research applied theoretical (social constructionist) and purposive strategies in choosing the sample. The parents came from all socio-economic groups, lived in different parts of the country, and had in common that they had given birth to or raised one or more child diagnosed with significant impairment (but various diagnostic labels) in a period of massive changes in social policy, law and the society. The sample was chosen because of its relevance to my research questions on parents' experiences of supports due to a disability in the family over time, and how the analytical framework and the explanations and narratives developed in the research.

In Iceland with its population of 319,000 people, like in any small community, it is inevitably hard to disguise any research informants. This can be almost impossible when researching the lives of disabled people and their families. This poses all kinds of ethical challenges related to trust and the protection of the identities of research participants.

Further, geographic and social proximity within such a small society invites other concerns like role conflicts both for the researcher, research assistants and the research participants. A number of times either I or my research assistant who came along to the interviews, had to turn away because one or the other of the parents to be interviewed turned out to be old friends or even in case of the research assistants, relations. In such cases either I or the research assistant (depending on which one of us did not know the people) took over the interview situation, or we dropped that family from the sample. Over-identification of the researcher with his or her research participants is another problem I was keenly aware of in this particular research, and in the process of the data analysis much of the data was coded independently by me and one of three research assistants. We then compared codes and notes and triangulated across and within cases.

ACCESS

Much has been written about problems researchers have had with gaining access to their field and getting past gate-keepers (e.g. Wolcott, 1994, 1995).

I have had problems getting access to research participants in the past, and was almost barred from a school by a powerful gate-keeper, who, halfway through the fieldwork, felt that the research was impinging upon the power relationships within the school. She was probably right. The research approach was action research. I did not have much experience in that nor did I realize the hegemony held by me in the eyes of the preschool teachers and other staff. My field notes from that study are filled with comments of stress and despair. The gate-keeper played me like a musical instrument, changing her tune, her rules and our agreement. I did manage to finish that research, after altering the research design several times, but my memories of that work are filled with pain, anger, surprise and more. This was amongst my most valuable lessons as a researcher, but I do not look back on the experience with pride.

In my more recent work including the family study referred to above, I have found it surprisingly easy to gain access. I am known in my society as both a parent of a disabled child, for a time active in the parents' movement, and as an academic. My university is also well known and respected. To gain access I simply called key people in the practical field of teaching or services for disabled people, explained in general terms what my research was about and enlisted their help to find suitable research participants. My contact people then contacted individuals who might be willing to talk to me, and after gaining their consent, sent me a list of names and phone numbers. I phoned these people, explained what I was doing and why and asked for interviews. We decided on a time and a place. In this study only one mother refused to give an interview. Two families had heard about my study. They contacted me and volunteered their stories. The willingness of parents (particularly the mothers) to participate in this research is gratifying but it also causes me concern. Many of the people I enlisted to help did so because they wanted to contribute their experiences in order to inform and enlighten professionals, politicians and the general public about the fate of their children, and thus combat stigmatization and prejudice. Each story is a unique gift. By accepting it, blurring individual details in the writing up process, publishing articles in academic journals, often in English, and using them in teaching, I must ask myself if I am taking these valuable gifts and applying them for my own ends? I am even more concerned when I learn that some of these parents have over the years been swamped with requests for interviews by students from upper secondary schools and universities, collecting material for their assignments, often with no preparation in interviewing technique.

Sigrun, a mother of a child with an unusual syndrome said, when I asked for an interview:

> It is OK; you can come because I know who you are. But I am getting a little tired of telling our story. Only this year I have contributed to at least nine or ten essays. I have never seen any of them...students just come with their questions about difficult aspects to our lives, tape my answers and leave. I never know what they do with the stuff. I want to help ...and I do it because I want young people to understand...but sometimes it is very difficult.

I found it somewhat more difficult to get some of the fathers to talk to me. But I tried to interview them without their wife or partner present. Typical explanations were; " I cannot find time", "I work away from home", "ask the wife, I know much less about what happens around my (disabled) child, she sees to all that and tells me if there is something I need to do". Sometimes a father has made an appointment to talk to me, but when I turned up he had gone to work or out on an errand, but his wife told me that I could always try later. This was problematic, particularly if the couple lived in a village or on a farm far away from the capital. This avoidance can mean a lot of things. It can be genuine, as many men feel compelled to work long hours, or because these fathers really believed they did not know enough about what was happening in their child's life, or did simply not want to talk about their experiences. The mothers seemed to trust in our shared experience, and many welcomed the opportunity to talk about their experiences to an insider. Some of the fathers may have found it difficult to talk to a woman and a stranger about experiences they did not talk about with friends or workmates and sometimes not even with their spouses. However, many appeared glad to talk to me. The fathers' stories were different from the mothers, and added important dimensions to my research. Some of these fathers, once agreeing to the interview, were putting words to experiences and feelings they had bottled up for a long time, and not even talked about with their partners. The role of the interviewer is not and should not be that of a therapist. But there is a fine line between listening to people's experiences and becoming their therapist. That line should not be crossed between the interviewer and the research participant. However, listening to the parents' narratives my eyes sometimes blurred. I learnt to keep a box of tissue within reach for the interviewees, but there is also a lot of smiley voices and laughter recorded and registered in the transcripts.

THE INTERVIEWS

The interviews took place either in my office or in the families' homes, depending on their preferences and the practicalities. The research had been certified by The National Bioethics Committee of Iceland and reported to The National Committee on the Protection and Processing of Personal Data. This is standard procedure under Icelandic law and the parents were reminded of this at the beginning of the interview when they co-signed a statement with me to that effect.

Building Rapport

I always began by explaining what I was doing without going into great detail. I talked about what the research was about, explained that I had a list of topics to talk about but not pre-designed questions, promised confidentiality, asked permission to record the interview, and answered any questions they had. I also told them that it was up to them what they chose to tell me and that we could stop the interview at any time. Further, that if they regretted what they had said later, I would erase the interview and not use it for the research purpose. Then we signed a paper of consent and confidentiality. All this is standard procedure.

I started the interview by asking about the family: "Tell me about the people in your family?" This question provided information on the family structure, number of children, the parents' work, education and previous marital status if applicable, the children's schooling and more. Most respondents found it easy to sketch out a brief description of their families, and the interview could move on.

The Interview

Next I asked the parent to describe their child (or in some cases children) labelled with disability, the child's strengths, personality, charm and needs. Most, but not all the parents used this question to draw up the strengths, abilities and charm of their child. The father of Peter, a 9 year old boy with Down's syndrome said:

> Peter is our eldest. He is absolutely delightful. He has developed allot in the past three to four years... kind of taken a big leap forward. He is good and gentle, and a surprisingly thinking human being... and he is almost able to read....He loves swimming and music and he loves people. He really is the sunshine in our lives...

A few parents however, answered my question by giving a detailed medical account of everything that was seen to be wrong with their child. One mother, Gudrun went as far as explaining to me using a Latin medical term which of her daughter's chromosomes was irregular, how that might have happened, and what the future prognosis might imply. She seemed surprised when I stooped her and asked her about her daughter's strengths and interests. She said with tears in her voice:

> She is lovely, of course, but nobody wants to know that. All people ask about is her problems.

I asked why she thought that might be so. She could not get a word out for a while, just cried. She said she did not know why she was crying, and I, handing her a tissue, offered to stop the interview; she declined and said she wanted to go on, but that she did not know why she was crying. Then she explained that when her daughter was born at the local hospital she was unable to suck, and Gudrun feared that maybe there was something wrong with her baby, but that the midwife blamed her and did not take her concern seriously. They were sent home, but when the baby was a few months old, it became undernourished. Gudrun had noticed that her baby did not move normally and became more and more frightened. Nobody believed her except her mother, and the midwife spread a story of Gudrun's incompetence as a mother. She was sent with her baby daughter by plane to the large teaching hospital in Reykjavík, and from there from one paediatrician to another. It was finally detected that her daughter had a regressive muscular disease. Once the expert had diagnosed the problem, she lost contact with him. She said:

> He was very busy. I do not blame him, but everything stopped. You are interesting while the diagnosis is being carried out, then when they have found out what is the matter, you are instantly forgotten.

Gudrun cried all through the interview, but declined my repeated offers to stop. She felt angry, betrayed by the midwife, the doctors, her husband, family and friends except for her own mother, who supported her. She needed to get all this off her chest. Interviews can be abusing. Was I opening a can of worms? For whom and to what end?

I am still not certain whether or not I should have gone on with the interview. My probing caused Gudrun to have to revisit some of the most difficult moments of her life. These were things she had not talked about for years, but when the memory came flowing back; it caused her a lot of pain. Was I using her trust and her story as a means to my research ends? How can I be sure she really wanted to do this? I think she felt my empathy and saw my tears reflect hers, but did that help or harm?

As mentioned in the introduction, the term *privileged knowledge* (Dianne Ferguson 2009) refers to some of the things the person being interviewed tells the interviewer, things that may be deeply private and personal, are not asked for and do not further the research. The researcher then has the privilege of that knowledge and the ethical dilemma of what to reveal and what to filter out in the analysis and the writing up. I have often been given the uneasy privilege of such knowledge. In the parent study, it did occur that a husband told me he was cheating on his wife with a woman in their circle of friends, that the marriage bed was getting cold because the wife was always too tired for making love, or the husband was unable to visit with his wife. I have even had to stop the car to cry or be sick after some such revelations. Knowledge of this kind is difficult to handle, especially if the researcher has to interview the other spouse, knowing what had been revealed. I chose to filter this kind of knowledge out before analysing the data.

The Data Analysis and the Writing up of Findings

In reading and rereading the data (in this example both the interviews and the research notes made at various stages of the analysis) it begins to speak to the researcher or the team of researchers in a new way. Themes begin to emerge within and between data bits. Triangulations have to be made both within and between cases, looking for similar and opposite examples. The research participants may have to be contacted for clarifications or verifications (Bogdan and Biklen, 20003).

In this process ethical issues creep in at every stage. What did he or she really mean, why did they skip this bit, lie about that, and what of all this can be written up, how and why? What is the researcher's big story about all these individual stories? The researcher must be cognizant that according to the interpretive (hermeneutic) social science there is a general acceptance that present experiences shape who we think we are and who we become. How we read our experiences and those reported by others is never what happened, but an outcome of a transaction between ourselves and the text. In the writing up and the publishing of the big story of the research there are more ethical issues. Questions such as; is this really respectful of the gifts you received from your research participants, is it trustworthy, and how will the readers eventually interoperate this piece of research, are they likely to use it, how and for what ends?

CONCLUSION

I have shared some of the many ethical issues and dilemmas confronting a qualitative researcher working with people in vulnerable situations. Many of these apply in all such research work, but call for extra care when the research participants are people whose voices are not generally heard or, if heard, taken seriously. I believe that it is the responsibility of the researcher in such cases to make as sure as possible that the research participants feel empowered through having shared their stories. It is also important to take the bigger story, the new understandings to the venue of policy makers, professionals, and the public, in the hope that new perspectives and new voices can throw a beam of light on the debate on how to use resources and what kind of society we might build for the future. If our work is to be taken seriously, it may well be controversial, but it has to be clear, ethical and open to scrutiny.

REFERENCES FOR ARTICLE

Barnes, C. (1991). *Disabled People in Britain and Discrimination.* London, Hust and Calgary.

Barnes, C. Mercer, G. and Shakespeare, T. (1999). *Exploring Disability: A Sociological Introduction.* Cambridge, Policy Press.

Bogdan, R. C. and Biklen, S.K.(2003). *Qualitative Research for Education. An Introductionto Theory and Methods.* 4th ed. New York, Pearson Education grp.

Bjarnason, D. S. (2002). New Voices in Iceland: Parents and adult children. Juggling supports and choices in time and space. *Disability and society* 17,3:307-327.

Bjarnason, D.S. (2003). School inclusion in Iceland: *The Cloak of Invisibility. In Education; Emerging Goals in a New Millennium*, B. T. Peck (editor), New York, Nova Science Publishers.

Bjarnason, D. S. (2004). New Voices from Iceland: Disability and Young Adulthood. New York, Nova Science Publishers.

Bjarnason, D.S. (2009). Parents and Professionals. An uneasy partnership? In J. Allan, J. Ozga and G. Smyth *Social Capital, Professionalism and Diversity: New Relations in Urban Schools.* Rotterdam: Sense Publishers.

Charlton, J. (2000). *Nothing about Us without Us: Disability, Oppression and Empowerment.* Berkeley, CA, University of California Press.

Christians, C. G. (2000). Ethics and politics in qualitative research. In Denzin, N.K. and Lincoln, Y.S. (edt.) *Handbook of qualitative research.* 2nd edition. Thousand Oaks. Sage publications: 133-155.

De Laine, M. (2000). *Fieldwork, participation and practice. Ethics and dilemmas in qualitative research.* London, Sage publications.

Disability and society. A Review Symposium. 22,2:230-234.

Ferguson, D.L. (2009). Personal communication.

Ferguson, P. (2001). Mapping the Family. Disability studies and the exploration of parental responses to disability. In G. L. Albrect, K. D. Seelman and M. Bury (Eds.) *Handbook of Disability Studies.*Thousand Oaks: Sage Publications: 373-395.

Ferguson, D.L. and Ferguson P.M. (1993). *The promise of Adulthood.* Columbus OH, Macmillan.

Ferguson, D. L. and Ferguson P. M. (1995). The interpretivist view of special education and disability: The value of telling stories. In T. M. Skrtic (ed.) *Disability and democracy: Reconstructing special education for postmodernity.* New York, Teachers College Press: 104-122.

Finch, J. (1984)" It's great to have someone to talk to": The ethics and politics of interviewing women. In C. Bell and H. Roberts (edt.) *Social Researching: Politics, problems and practice.* London, Routledge and Kegan, Paul. :70-87

Oakeley, A. (1979). *Becoming a Mother.* Oxford: Martin Robertson.

Oakeley, A. (1981). *Subject Women.* Oxford: Martin Robertson. New York, Pantheon.

O'Brien, R. (2001). *Crippled Justice: The History of Modern Disability Policy in the Workplace.* Chicago, University of Chicago Press.

Oliver, M. (1990). *The politics of Disablement: Critical Texts in Social Work and the Welfare State.* Basingstoke, Macmillan.

Oliver, M. (1996). *Understanding Disability: From Theory to Practice.* Basingstoke, Macmillan.

Oliver, M. (2007) . Review Symposium, *Disability and society*,22,2:232-234.

Punch, M. (1998). Politics and ethics in qualitative research. In Denzin, N.K.and Lincoln (edt.) *The landscape of qualitative research*: *Theories and issues.* Thousand Oakes, Sage Publications. : 156-184.

Schwandt, T. A. (2001). Dictionary of Qualitative Inquiry (2nd edt.). Thousand Oakes, Sage Publications.

Shakespeare, T. (2006). *Disability Rights and Wrongs.* London, Rouledge. Homepage:www.sahealthinfo.org/ethics/ethicsqualitative.htm. Retrieved 15th April 2009.

Skrtic T. M. (ed.) (1995). *Disability and Democracy: Reconstructing Special Education for Postmodernity*. New York, Teachers College Press: 104-122.

Turnbull A. and Turnbull, R. (edt.) (2005). *Families, Professionals and Exceptionality* . New York, Prentice Hall.

Vehmas, S. (2008). Philosophy and Science: The Axes of Evil in Disability Studies? *Journal of Medical Ethics*, 34:21-23.

White, T. (1993). Business Ethics: A Philosophical Reader. New York, Macmillan

Wolcott, H.F. (1994).*Transforming Qualitative Data. Description, Analysis, and Interpretation*. Thousand Oakes, Sage Publications.

Wolcott, H.F. (1995). *The Art of Fieldwork*. Walnut Creek, Alta Mira Press.

REFERENCES

Albrecht, G. L., Seelman, K. D., and Bury, M. (Eds.). (2001). *Handbook of disability studies*. Thousand Oaks: Sage.

Allan, J. (1999). *Actively seeking inclusion: Pupils with special needs in mainstream schools.* London: Falmer.

Allan, J., Buckel, C., Catts, R., Doherty, R., McDonald, A., McGonigal, J., et al. (2005). *Social capital theory: A review.* Retrieved May 7, 2010 from http://www.aers.org.uk/dspace/handle/123456789/19

Allan, J., Ozga, J., and Smith, G. (Eds.). (2009). *Social capital, professionalism and diversity* (Vol. 1). Rotterdam: Sense Publishers.

Alþingistíðindi (1992). 115 löggjafarþing. 222. mál, félagsmálarh. (Jóhanna Sigurðardóttir): málefni fatlaðra 1. umræða [Social affairs minister´s speech in parliament on the affairs of persons with disabilities]. Retrieved May 13, 2010 from http://www.althingi.is/altext/115/02/r19135000.sgml

Alþingistíðindi (1991). 115. löggjafarþing. 20. mál. Frumvarp til laga um málefni fatlaðra. , [Legal bill for the affairs of persons with disabilities: Presented in Althing on the 115th congress]. Retrieved May 12, 2010 from http://www.althingi.is/altext/133/s/0020.html

Anonymous (1951). When a child is different. In W. C. Kveraceus and E. N. Hayes (Eds.), *If your child is handicapped*. Boston: Porter Sargent

Baldursdóttir, Á. (2008, June, 13). "Ég er örmagna" ["I am exhausted"]. *24 stundir,* pp. 1 and 8. Retrieved May 10, 2010 from http://timarit.is/view_page_init.jsp?pageId=3628927.

Berger, P. L. (1963). *Invitation to Sociology: A humanistic perspective.* Garden City, N.Y.: Doubleday.

Berger, P. L., and Luckman, T. (1967). *The social construction of reality: A treatise in the sociology of knowledge*. London: Penguin.

Bérubé, M. (1996). *Life as We Know It: A Father, a family, and an exceptional child.* New York: Pantheon.

Bjarnadóttir, R. I., Garðarsdóttir, G., Smárason, A. K., and Pálsson, G. E. (2008). *Skýrsla frá fæðingaskráningunni fyrir árið 2007 [Annual report from the Icelandic birth registration, 2007].* Reykjavík: Landspítaliháskólasjúkrahús.

Bjarnason, D. S. and Persson, B. (2007). Inkludering i de nordiska utbildningssystemen - en sociohistorisk bakgrund [Inclusion in the Nordic educational systems - A sociohistorical background]. *Psykologisk Pædagogisk Raadgivning. Tema: Inkluderende Pædagogik i Norden, 44*(3), 202-224.

Bjarnason, D. S. (1996). Iceland: From institutions to normalisation? In J. Tøssebro, A. Gustavsson and G. Dyrendahl (Eds.), *Intellectual disabilities in the Nordic welfare states* (pp. 237). Kristiansand: Høyeskoleforlaget.

Bjarnason, D. S. (2002). New voices in Iceland: Parents and adult children: Juggling supports and choices in time and space. *Disability and Society, 17*(3), 307-326.

Bjarnason, D. S. (2003). *School inclusion in Iceland: The cloak of invisibility.* New York: Nova Science.

Bjarnason, D. S. (2004). *New voices from Iceland: Disability and young adulthood.* New York: Nova Science.

Bjarnason, D. S. (2009a). Parents and professionals: An uneasy partnership. In J. Allan, J. Ozga, G. Smith (Eds.), *Social capital, professionalism and diversity.* Rotterdam: Sense Publishers.

Bjarnason, D. S. (2009b). Walking on eggshells: Some ethical issues in research with people in vulnerable situations. *Educare, 2009*(4), 19-34.

Bjarnason, D. S. (2010). Raddir foreldra fatlaðra barna: Reynsla af stuðningi Tryggingastofnunar vegna fötlunar barns á tímabilinu 1974-2008 [Voices of parents of children with disabilities: Experience of support from the State social insurance, on account of a childs disability]. *Þroskahjálp, 32*(1), 10-16.

Bjarnason, D. S. (in print). Gjennom labyrinten: Hva er (spesial) pedagogikk i et inkluderende miljø? [Through the Maze: What is (special-) education in inclusive settings?]. In S. Reindahl and R. S. Hausstätter (Eds.), *Spesialpedagogikk og etikk: Kollektivt ansvar og individuelle rettigheter [Special education and ethics: Collective responsibility and individual rights].* Lillehammer: Høyskoleforlaget.

Bogdan, R., and Biklen, S. K. (1992). *Qualitative research for education: An introduction to theory and methods.* (2nd ed.). Boston: Allyn and Bacon.

Bogdan, R. C., and Biklen, S. K. (2003). *Qualitative research for education: An introduction to theories and methods*. (4th ed.). New York: Pearson Education.

Booth, T. (1978). From a normal baby to handicapped child: Unravelling the idea of subnormality in families of mentally handicapped children. *Sociology, 12*, 203-221.

Bourdieu, P. (1984). *Distinction: A social critique of the judgement of taste* (R. Nice, trans.). London: Routledge and Kegan Paul. (Original publication 1979)

Bourdieu, P. (1986). The forms of capital. In J. Richardson (Ed.), *Handbook of theory and research for the sociology of education* (pp. 241-258). Westport, Ct: Greenwood Press.

Campbell, C., Catts, R., Gallagher, M., Livingston, K., and Smyth, G. (2005). *Social capital research literature: A preliminary review*. Retrieved May 12, 2010 from www.aers.org.uk/dspace/retrieve/18/FINALpaper.doc

Coleman, J. S. (1994). *Foundations of social theory*. Cambridge: Beknap Press.

Deild fyrir einhverf börn stofnuð í haust [A special class for autistic children established in the autumn] (2009, September 1). *Fréttablaðið*. Retrieved June 2, 2010 from http://www.visir.is/article/20090901/FRETTIR01/926915102.

Dillenburger, K., Keenan, M., Doherty, A., Byrne, T., and Gallagher, S. (2010). Living with children diagnosed with autistic spectrum disorder: Parental and professional views. *British Journal of Special Education, 37*(1), 13-23.

Edelstein, W. (1988). *Skóli, nám, samfélag [School, learning, community]*. Reykjavík: Iðunn.

Ferguson, D. L., and Ferguson, P. M. (1993). The promise of adulthood. In M. Snell (Ed.), *Instrucion of students with severe disabilities*. Columbus, OH: Macmillan.

Ferguson, D. L., and Ferguson, P. M. (1995). The interpretivist view of special education and disability: The value of telling stories. In T. M. Skrtic (Ed.), *Disability and democracy: Reconstructing special education for postmodernity* (pp. 104-122). New York: Teachers College Press.

Ferguson, D. L., Ferguson, P. M., and Jones, D. (1988). Generations of hope: Parental perspectives on transitions of their severely retarded children from school to adult life. *Journal of the Association for Persons with Severe Handicaps, 13*, 177-186.

Ferguson, P. M. (2001, October). *Winks, blinks, squints and twitches: Looking for disability and culture through my son's left eye*. Paper presented at the NNDR conference, Copenhagen. [In print in Nordic Journal of Disability Research].

Ferguson, P. M. (1994). *Abandoned to their fate: Social policy and practice toward severely retarded people in America, 1820-1920*. Philadelphia: Temple University Press.

Ferguson, P. M. (2001a). Mapping the family: Disability studies and the exploration of parental response to disability. In G. L. Albrecht, K. D. Seelman and M. Bury (Eds.), *Handbook of disability studies*. Thousand Oaks: Sage

Ferguson, P. M. (2008). The doubting dance: Contributions to a history of parent/professional interactions in early 20th century America. *Research and Practice for Persons with Severe Disabilities (RPSD), 33*(1), 48-58.

Ferguson, P. M., and Ash, A. (1989). Lessons from life: Personal and parental perspectives on school, childhood and disability. In D. P. Biklen, D. L. Ferguson and A. Ford (Eds.), *Schooling and disability: Eighty-eight yearbook of the National Society for the Study of Education.* (Vol. II, pp. 10140). Chicago: National Society for the Study of Education.

Félags- og tryggingamálaráðuneytið (2008). *Yfirstjórn málefna aldraðra og almannatrygginga í nýju félags- og tryggingamálaráðuneyti [Administration of the affairs of the elderly and social security by a new Ministry of Social Affairs and Social Security]*. Retrieved December 12, 2008, from http://www.felagsmalaraduneyti.is/frettir/frettatilkynningar/nr/3618.

Félags- og tryggingamálaráðuneytið (e.d.a). *Félags- og tryggingamálaráðuneytið [Ministry of Social Affairs and Social Security]*, homepage. Retrieved July 20, 2008, from http://www. felagsmalaraduneyti.is/.

Félags- og tryggingamálaráðuneytið (e.d.b). *Félags- og tryggingamálaráðuneytið [Ministry of Social Affairs and Social Security]*, homepage. Retrieved May 4, 2009, from http://www. felagsmalaraduneyti.is/

Félags- og tryggingamálaráðuneytið (e.d.c). Félags- og tryggingamálaráðuneytið [Ministry of Social Affairs and Social Security], homepage. Retrieved May 3, 2010, from http://www. felagsmalaraduneyti.is/.

Field, J. (2003). *Social capital*. London: Routledge.

Forsætisráðuneytið (2008*). Könnun á starfsemi Breiðavíkurheimilisins 1952-1979: Skýrsla nefndar samkvæmt lögum nr.26/2007 [Investigation of the *activities of the Breidavik home 1952-1979. A commitee report according to Act No. 26/2007].* Retrieved May 11, 2010 from http://www.for saetisraduneyti.is/media/Skyrslur/Breidavikurskyrsla.pdf.

Forsætisráðuneytið (2009). *Skýrsla nefndar samkvæmt lögum nr. 26/2007, áfangaskýrsla nr.1: Könnun á starfasemi Heyrnleysingjaskólans 1947-1992, vistheimilisins Kumbaravogs 1965-1984 og skólaheimilisins Bjargs 1965-1967 [Commitee report according to Act No. 26/2007, progress report nr. 1: Investigation of the activities of the School for the deaf, 1947-1992, the institution at Kumbaravogur, 1965-1984, and the boarding school at Bjarg, 1965-1967].* Retrieved May 10, 2010, from http://www.forsaetisraduneyti.is/media/Skyrslur/2009-09-afangaskyrsla1-konnun-barnaheimila.pdf.

Foucault, M. (1975). *The Birth of the clinic: An archaeology of medical perception* (A. M. S. Smith, trans.). New York: Vintage books. (Original publication 1963).

Fræðsluráð Reykjavíkur (2002). *Stefna fræðsluráðs Reykjavíkur um sérkennslu [Reykjavík's education council's policy in special education].* Reykjavík: Fræðslumiðstöð Reykjavíkur.

Gabel, S. (2001). Problems of methodology in cross-cultural disability studies: A South-Asian-Indian example. *Exploring Theories and Expanding Methodologies, 2,* 209-223.

Gallimore, R., Weisner, T. S., Kaufman, S. Z., and Bernheimer, L. P. (1989). The social construction of ecocultural niches: Family accommodation of developmentally delayed children. *American Journal on Mental Retardation, 94,* 216-230.

Geirsson, R. T. (2001). Ómsskoðun við 18 - 20 vikur [Ultrasound scanning at 18 - 20 weeks]. *Læknablaðið, 87,* 403-407. Retrieved May 13, 2010 from http://www.laeknabladid.is/2001/5/fraedigreinar//nr/896/

Gergen, K. J. (1994). *Realities and relationships: Soundings in social construction.* Cambrigde, Mass.: Harvard University Press.

Getz, L., and Kirkengen, A. L. (2003). Ultrasound screening in pregnancy: Advancing technology, soft markers for fetal chromosomal aberrations, and unaknowledged ethical dilemmas. *Social Science and Medicine, 56,* 2045-2057.

Giddens, A. (1993). *Sociology.* (2nd. ed.). Oxford: Blackwell.

Giddens, A. (2001). *Sociology* (4th ed.). Cambridge: Polity Press

Gísladóttir, H. (2007). *Nám á starfsbraut í framhaldsskóla: Undirbúningur fyrir fullorðinsár [Vocational course of study in upper secondary school:*

Preparation for adulthood]. Unpublished M.Ed. dissertation. Kennaraháskóli Íslands.

Glaser, B., and Strauss, A. L. (1967). *The discovery of grounded theory: Strategies for qualitative research.* Chicago: Aldine.

Goodley, D. (2007). Becoming rhizomatic parents: Deleuze, Guattari and disabled babies. *Disability and Society, 22*(2), 145-160.

Goodley, D., and Lawthom, R. (2008). Disability studies and psychology: Emancipatory opportunities. In S. Gabel and S. Danforth (Eds.), *Disability Studies in Education: A Reader.* New York: Peter Lang.

Greiningar- og ráðgjafarstöð ríkisins (e.d.a). *Greiningar- og ráðgjafarstöð ríkisins [The State Diagnostic and Counselling Centre (SDCC)],* homepage. Retrieved July 10, 2009, from http://www.greining.is/

Greiningar- og ráðgjafarstöð ríkisins (e.d.b). *Greiningar- og ráðgjafarstöð ríkisins [The State Diagnostic and Counselling Centre (SDCC)],* homepage. Retrieved July 15, 2009, from http://www.greining.is/

Gunnlaugsson, G. Á. (1982). *Ómagar og utangarðsfólk: Fátækramál Reykjavíkur 1786-1907 [Paupers and outsiders in Reykjavík 1786-1907].* Reykjavík: Sögufélag.

Gunnlaugsson, G. Á. (1997). Fátækt í íslensku samfélagi [Poverty in Icelandic society]. In G. Hálfdánarson, L. Guttormsson and Ó. Garðarsdóttir (Eds.), *Saga og samfélag: Þættir úr félagssögu 19. og 20. aldar [History and community: Episodes from the social history of the 19th and 20th century].* Reykjavík: Sagnfræðistofnun Háskóla Íslands.

Guttormsson, L. (1983). *Bernska, ungdómur og uppeldi á einveldisöld: Tilraun til félagslegrar og lýðfræðilegrar greiningar [Childhood, youth and upbringing: An attempt to a sociological and demographic analysis].* Reykjavík: Sagnfræðistofnun Háskóla Íslands.

Guttormsson, L. (2008). Fyrsti hluti. Hefðir og nýbreytni 1880-1907 [Traditions and novelty 1880-1907]. In L. Guttormsson (Ed.), *Almenningsfræðsla á Íslandi 1880-2007[Public education in Iceland 1880-2007]* (Vol. 1, pp. 21-69). Reykjavík: Háskólaútgáfan.

Hagstofa Íslands (e.d.a). *Heilbrigðis-, félags- og dómsmál [Health, social affairs and justice].* Retrieved January 20, 2009, from http://hagstofa.is/Hagtolur/Heilbrigdis,-felags-og-domsmal

Hagstofa Íslands (e.d.b). *Þjóðhagsreikningar [National accounts].* Retrieved May 12, 2010, from http://www.hagstofa.is/pages/983#11.4

Heilbrigðisráðuneytið (e.d). *Sjúkrahús og heilbrigðisstofnanir [Hospitals and health institutions].* Retrieved May 10, 2010, from http://www.heilbr igdisraduneyti.is/stofnanir/sjukrahus_og_heilbrigdisstofnanir/

Heilsugæsla höfuðborgarsvæðisins (e.d.). *Ungbarnavernd [Infant care]*. Retrieved June 29, 2009, from http://www.heilsugaeslan.is/?PageID=282

Herbertsson, T. Ó. (2005). *Fjölgun öryrkja á Íslandi. Orsakir og afleiðingar [Increase in the number of people on disability pension in Iceland: Causes and consequences]*. Reykjavik: Heilbrigðis og tryggingamálaráðuneytið.

Jarlsdóttir, H. E. (2008). Gleymdust börnin okkar í góðærinu? [Were our children forgotten in the economic boom?]. *Víkurfréttir*, (24).

Jóhannesson, G. T. (2009). *Hrunið: Ísland á barmi gjaldþrots og upplausnar [The collapse: Iceland on the verge of bankrupcy and dissolution]*. Reykjavík: JPV.

Jóhannesson, I. Á. (2006). Strong, independent, able to learn more: Inclusion and the construction of school students in Iceland as diagnosable subjects. *Discource: Studies in the Cultural Politics of Education, 27*(1), 103-119.

Jónasson, J. T. (2008). Skóli fyrir alla? [School for everyone?] In L. Guttormsson (Ed.), *Almenningsfræðsla á Íslandi 1880-2007* [Public education in Iceland 1880-2007] (Vol. 2, pp. 272-291). Reykjavík: Háskólaútgáfan.

Jónsson, G. (2009). Efnahagskreppur á Íslandi 1870-2000 [Economic crises in Iceland 1870-2000]. *Saga, XLVII*(2), 45-74.

Kirkebæk, B. (2001). *Normaliserings periode: Dansk ådssvageforsorg 1940-1970 med særligt fokus på forsorgschef N. E. Mikkelsen og udviklingen af Statens Åndssvageforsorg 1959-1970 [The normalization period: Danish care for intellectually disabled people 1940-1970]*.

Kirkebæk, B. (2007). *Uduelig og ubrugelig: Åndssvageasylet Karens Minde 1880-1987[Incapable and useless: Karens Minde asylum for the mentally retarded 1880-1987]*. Holte: SocPol.

Kirkebæk, B., Clausen, H., Storm, K., and Dyssegaard, B. (1994). *Skrøbelig kontakt: For tidligt födte börn og deres samspil med omgivelserne [Fragile interaction: Premature babies and their interaction with the environment]*. København: Dansk psykologisk Forlag.

Kristoffersen, G. (1988). *Hvordan påvirker et handicappet barn familien psykisk og socialt? [How does a diabled child affect the family, psychically and socially?]*. København: Author.

Landlæknisembættið (2008). Meðgönguvernd heilbrigðra kvenna í eðlilegri meðgöngu: Klíniskar leiðbeiningar [Prenatal care for healthy women during normal pregnancy: Clinical instructions]. Retrieved May 13, 2010 from http://www.landlaeknir.is/lisalib/getfile.aspx?itemid=3607

Lundeby, H., and Tøssebro, J. (2008a). Family structure in Norwegian families of children with disabilities. *Journal of Applied Research in Intellectual Disabilities, 21*(3), 246-256.

Lundeby, H., and Tøssebro, J. (2008b). The Experiences of "Not being listened to" from the perspective of parents with disabled children. *Scandinavian Journal of Disability Research 10*(4), 558-575.

Lög um aðstoð við þroskahefta nr. 47/1979 [Act No. 47/1979 on assistance to the mentally retarded].

Lög um almannatryggingar nr.100/2007 [Act No. 100/2007 on social security].

Lög um almannatryggingar nr. 67/1971 [Act No. 67/1971 on social security].

Lög um almannatryggingar nr. 117/1993 [Act No. 117/1993 on social security].

Lög um alþýðutryggingar nr. 26/1936 [Act No. 26/1936 on social security].

Lög um breyting á lögum um grunnskóla nr. 66/1995, nr. 77/1996 [Act No. 77/1996 amending Act No. 66/1995 on compulsory schools].

Lög um breytta verkaskiptingu ríkis og sveitarfélaga nr. 87/1989 [Act on a changed division of labour between government and municipalities].

Lög um félagsþjónustu sveitarfélaga nr. 40/1991 [Act No. 40/1991 on municipalities' social services].

Lög um framhaldsskóla nr. 92/2008 [Act No. 92/2008 on colleges].

Lög um framhaldsskóla nr. 80/1996 [Act No. 80/1996 on colleges].

Lög um fæðingar- og foreldraorlof nr. 95/2000 [Act No. 95/2000 on maternity and parental leave].

Lög um Greiningar- og ráðgjafarstöð ríkisins nr. 83/2003 [Act No. 83/2003 on The State Diagnostic and Counselling Centre].

Lög um grunnskóla nr. 49/1991 [Act No. 49/1991 on compulsory schools].

Lög um grunnskóla nr. 91/2008 [Act No. 91/2008 on compulsory schools].

Lög um heilbrigðisþjónustu nr. 40/2007 [Act No. 40/2007 on health services].

Lög um heyrnleysingjaskóla nr. 13/1962 [Act No. 13/1962 on a school for the deaf].

Lög um hlutdeild ríkisins í byggingu og rekstri dagvistunarheimila nr. 29/1973 [Act No. 29/1973 on the government's part in constructing and operating day-care centers].

Lög um leikskóla nr. 78/1994 [Act No. 78/1994 on preschools].

Lög um leikskóla nr. 90/2008 [Act No. 90/2008 on preschools].

Lög um málefni fatlaðra nr. 41/1983 [Act No. 41/1983 on the affairs of persons with disabilities].

Lög um málefni fatlaðra nr. 59/1992 [Act No. 59/1992 on the affairs of persons with disabilities].

Lög um reynslusveitarfélög nr. 82/1994 [Act No. 82/1994 on experimental municipalities].

Margeirsdóttir, M. (1975). *Könnun á fjölda vangefinna og skipting þeirra eftir landshlutum[A report on the number of people with developmental disability and their division in different administrational areas of Iceland]*. Reykjavík: Heilbrigðis- og tryggingamálaráðuneytið.

Margeirsdóttir, M. (2001). *Fötlun og samfélag [Disability and society]*. Reykjavík: Háskólaútgáfan.

Marinósson, G. L. (Ed.) (2007). *Tálmar og tækifæri. Menntun nemenda með þroskahömlun á Íslandi [Hindrances and opportunities: The education of students with developmental disabilities in Iceland]*. Reykjavík: Háskólaútgáfan.

Mark, M. E., Hallgrímsdóttir, M., and Ingólfsson, E. F. (2007). *Undrabörn / Exeptional children* (A. Sigmundsdóttir and H. S. Einarsdóttir, trans.). Reykjavík: Þjóðminjasafn Íslands.

McLaughlin, J., Goodley, D., Clavering, E., and Fisher, P. (2008). *Families raising disabled children: Enabling care and social justice*. London: Palgrave Macmillan.

Ministry of Education, Science and Culture (2002). *The educational system in Iceland*. Reykjavík: Ministry of Education, Science and Culture.

Ministry of Health (e.d.). *Information about the Icelandic health care system*. Retrieved January 20, 2009, from http://eng.heilbrigd israduneyti.is/Information/nr/677

Morthens, A. (2009). An interview with Arthur Morthens conducted by author on the 14th of May.

NOMESCO (2008). *Health statistics in the Nordic countries 2006*. Retrieved May 20, 2010 from http://nomesco-eng.nom-nos.dk/filer/publik ationer/Helse%202006.pdf

O'Connor, S. (1995). More than what they bargained for: The meaning of support to families. In S. J. Taylor, R. C. Bogdan and Z. M. Lutfiyya (Eds.), *The variety of community experience: Qualitative studies of family and community life*. Baltimore, MD: Paul H. Brookes Publishing.

Oliver, M. (1990). *The politics of disablement*. Basingstoke: Macmillan.

Ólafsson, S. (1999). *Íslenska leiðin [The Icelandic way]*. Reykjavík: Tryggingastofnun ríkisins.

Ólafsson, S. (2005). *Örorka og velferð á Íslandi og í öðrum vestrænum löndum [Disability and welfare in Iceland and other western countries]*.

Reykjavík: Félagsvísindastofnun Háskóla Íslands, Öryrkjabandalag Íslands.

Ólafsson, S., and Jónsson, F. H. (1991). *Lífsskoðun í nútímalegum þjóðfélögum: Samanburður á Íslendingum, Dönum, Finnum, Norðmönnum, Svíum, öðrum Evrópuþjóðum og Bandaríkjamönnum [View of life in modern societies: Comparison of Icelanders, Danes, Finns, Norwegians, Swedes, other European nations and Americans].* Reykjavík: Félagsvísindastofnun.

Putnam, R. D. (1995). Bowling alone: America, declining social capital. *Journal of Democracy, 6*(1), 65-78.

Putnam, R. D. (2000). *Bowling alone: The collapse and revival of American community.* New York: Simon and Schuster.

Ragnarsdóttir, H. (2005). *Tilfærsla fatlaðra ungmenna úr skóla yfir í atvinnulíf [Transference of youngsters with disabilities from school to employment].* Unpublished M.Ed. dissertation. Kennaraháskóli Íslands.

Reglugerð um jöfnunarframlög Jöfnunarsjóðs sveitarfélaga til reksturs grunnskóla nr. 351/2002 [Regulations No. 351/2002 on municipalities compensation contributions to compulsory schools].

Reglugerð um sérkennslu nr. 270/1977 [Regulations No. 270/1977 on special education].

Reglugerð um Stjórnarráð Íslands nr. 177/2007 [Regulations No. 177/2007 on the goverment offices of Iceland].

Reid, D. K., and Button, L. J. (1995). Anna's story: Narratives of personal experience about being labeled learning disabled. *Journal of Learning Disabilities, 28*(10), 602-615.

Rix, J. (2003). A parents wish-list. In M. Nind, K..Sheehy, J. Rix, K. Simmons, (Eds.), *Inclusive education: Diverse perspectives.* London: David Fulton.

Schaefer, N. (1982). *Does she know she's there?* Toronto: Fitzhenry and Whiteside.

Schwandt, T. A. (2001). *Dictionary of qualitative enquiry.* Thousand Oaks: Sage.

Sigurðardóttir, A. K. (2009). Rannsóknir - eða trúboð?: Yfirlýsing frá Önnu Kristínu Sigurðardóttur og Ingólfi Ásgeiri Jóhannessyni [Research or missionary work?: Statements from Sigurðardóttir and Jóhannesson]. *Þroskahjálp, 31*(1), 29.

Sigurðsson, F. (2010). An interview with Friðrik Sigurðsson conducted by author.

Sigurðsson Þ. (1993). *Þættir úr sögu sérkennslunnar [Episodes from the history of special education]* (new ed.). Reykjavík: Þórsútgáfan.

Sætersdal, B. (1997). Integrering og mentalitetshistorie: Familieperspektiv på skiftende ideologier [Integration and mental history: The family perspective on various ideologies]. In J. Tøssebro (Ed.), *Den vanskelige integreringen [The problematic integration]* (pp. 181-196). Oslo: Universitetsforlaget.

Taylor, S. J., and Bogdan, R. (1984). *Introduction to qualitative research and methods: The search for meaning.* New York: Wiley.

Titmuss, R. M. (1974). *Social policy: An introduction.* New York: Pantheon Books.

Tryggingastofnun ríkisins (e.d.a). *General Information.* Retrieved June 26, 2009, from http://www.tr.is/english

Tryggingastofnun ríkisins (e.d.b). *Greiðslur vegna barna [Child support payments].* Retrieved May 12, 2010, from http://www.tr.is/foreldrar-og-born/greidslur/

Tryggingastofnun ríkisins (e.d.c). *Tryggingastofnun ríkisins [State social security],* homepage. Retrieved July 23, 2008, from http://www.tr.is/

Turnbull, A. P., and Turnbull, H. R. (1997). *Families, professionals and exceptionality: A special partnership.* (3rd ed.). Upper Saddle River, N.J.: Merrill.

Tøssebro, J. (2002). *A brief introduction to "the Nordic relational approach to disability".*
Paper presented at the 6th NNDR annual conference.

Tøssebro, J., and Lundeby, H. (2002). *Å vokse opp med funksjonshemming. De første årene [Growing up with disability: The first years].* Oslo: Gyldendal akademisk.

United Nations (1994). *The Salamanca statement and framework for action on special needs education: Adopted by The world conference on special needs education: Access and quality, Salamanca, Spain, 7-10 June 1994.* Paris: Unesco.

United Nations (2006). Convention on the rights of persons with disabilities. Retrieved May 13, 2010, from http://www.un.org/disabilities/convention/conventionfull.shtml

Valle, J. W. (2009). *What mothers say about special education: From the 1960s to the present*: Palgrave Macmillan.

Wittgenstein, L. (1958). *Philosophical investigation.* (3rd ed.). New York: Macmillan.

Wolcott, H. F. (1994). *Transforming qualitative data: Description, analysis and interpretation.* London: Sage.

Wolcott, H. F.(1995). *The art of fieldwork.* Walnut Creek: Sage.

World Health Organization (1992). *The ICD-10 classification of mental and behavioural disorders: Clinical descriptions and diagnostic guidelines.* Geneva: World Health Organization.

World Health Organization (1993). *The ICD-10 classification of mental and behavioural disorders: Diagnostic criteria for research.* Geneva: World Health Organization.

World Health Organization (2001). *The international classification of functioning, disability and health: ICF.* Geneva: World Health Organization.

World Health Organization (2006). *The international classification of functioning, disability and health, children and youth version: ICF-CY.* Geneva: World Health Organization.

Ytterhus, B., Wendelborg, C., and Lundeby, H. (2008). Managing turning points and transitions in childhood and parenthood - insights from families with disabled children in Norway. *Disability and Society, 23*(6), 625-636.

Þorláksson, E., Hjaltason, P., and Sigurðardóttir, S. (2008). Trúboðið um skóla án aðgreiningar: Nokkur varnarorð [The mission for school inclusion: A few words of caution]. *Þroskahjálp, 30*(1), 15-18.

INDEX

A

abortion, 85, 88, 90, 91, 92, 93, 94, 95, 96, 111
abuse, 99, 140
accessibility, 75
accommodation, 47, 161
accountability, 37, 146
accuracy, 52
action research, 148
adaptations, 106
ADHD, 77, 78
administrators, 14, 46, 111, 123
adulthood, 45, 86, 99, 118, 158, 159, 162
advocacy, 4, 41, 56, 72, 73, 74, 82, 112
affluence, 25
agencies, 34, 40
amniocentesis, 85
analytical framework, 148
anchoring, 22
anger, 65, 101, 109, 148
anthropology, 46
anxiety, 8, 89
architecture, 17, 105
arousal, 63
Asia, 61
assessment, 4, 8, 9, 12, 13, 22, 23, 37, 58, 64, 75, 100
asylum, 55, 163
atrophy, 99

authenticity, 52
authorities, viii, 23, 32, 37, 41, 57, 71, 72, 76, 77, 78, 111
autism, 3, 7, 9, 10, 39, 76, 77, 78, 98, 99, 100, 101, 102, 105, 112, 117, 122

B

bankers, 110, 130
bleeding, 87
blindness, 39, 98, 99
brain, 87, 91, 99
brain damage, 99
breastfeeding, 61
breathing, 86
Britain, 130, 154
brothers, 90
buildings, 106
bureaucracy, 10, 25, 67, 79
burnout, 127

C

caesarean section, 11
category b, 107
cerebral palsy, 8
certificate, 68
charm, 51, 114, 151
child protection, 41
childcare, 115
childhood, 73, 92, 95, 99, 100, 113, 160, 168

chronic diseases, 56
chronic illness, 37
citizenship, 56
City, 107, 157
civil society, 20
class, 8, 10, 17, 30, 70, 72, 78, 107, 127, 130, 159
clients, 99
climate, 2, 53, 115, 128, 131
clinical psychology, 26
coffee, 50, 84, 101, 122
colleges, 164
color, iv
community, 3, 6, 11, 12, 14, 20, 32, 36, 56, 69, 100, 106, 122, 124, 125, 128, 130, 134, 148, 159, 162, 165, 166
community service, 32
community support, 36
community-based services, 56
compassion, 92, 97, 101, 113
compensation, 166
complaints, 62, 103, 104
complications, 12, 14, 61
compulsory education, 31, 32, 34, 58, 70, 105, 107
conference, 160, 167
confidentiality, 50, 151
conflict, 20, 116, 123, 144
consensus, 42, 63
consent, 46, 50, 145, 149, 151
consumption, 115
convention, 167
cost, 28, 32, 41, 57, 69, 74, 97, 105, 111, 115, 125
cotton, 63
credentials, 27
creep, 153
crew, 113, 116
cultural studies, 19
culture, 22, 69, 99, 117, 144, 160
cycles, vii, 3

D

dance, 126, 160
danger, 52, 114, 131

data analysis, xi, 18, 52, 53, 140, 141, 147, 148
data collection, 46, 52
data gathering, xi
database, 46, 147
deaths, 121
deconstruction, 20
degradation, 63
democracy, 155, 159
demonstrations, 21
denial, 109, 112, 119
developmental disorder, 42
developmental milestones, 8
diagnosis, ix, 9, 22, 39, 42, 46, 63, 64, 65, 67, 69, 77, 82, 83, 84, 89, 97, 98, 100, 102, 104, 118, 119, 121, 125, 152
diplomacy, 10
disappointment, 78, 80
disorder, 81, 99, 100, 159
diversification, 41
diversity, 46, 142, 157, 158
doctors, 42, 43, 59, 60, 62, 63, 64, 82, 86, 88, 90, 99, 100, 123, 124, 129, 152
drawing, 107, 121
dyslexia, 105, 106

E

earnings, 6
Easter, 118
Eastern Europe, 83
economic boom, 2, 77, 93, 114, 163
economic change, 1
economic growth, 79, 130
economy, 2, 26, 79, 131
educational policy, 105
educational programs, 33
educational research, 140
educational services, 14, 70, 108
educational system, 26, 31, 46, 49, 105, 158, 165
empathy, 146, 152
employment, 2, 79, 130, 166
encouragement, 23, 72
entrepreneurs, 141
epilepsy, 83, 84

epistemology, 19, 144, 146
equipment, 37, 59, 69, 108, 125
equity, 78, 107
erosion, 130, 146
ethical issues, 53, 139, 140, 143, 144, 145, 153, 154, 158
ethical standards, 144, 146
ethics, 3, 19, 45, 139, 140, 143, 144, 145, 155, 158
ethnicity, 17
EU, 2
evil, 95
exaggeration, 103
examinations, 60
exclusion, 141, 142, 146
exercise, 20, 124
experiences, xi, 1, 2, 3, 4, 10, 14, 15, 19, 20, 21, 46, 47, 51, 53, 59, 73, 96, 100, 101, 127, 128, 139, 140, 142, 144, 145, 147, 149, 150, 153
expertise, 10, 64, 125
exploitation, 146
exploration, 155, 160

F

facial expression, 61
family life, v, 3, 17, 18, 21, 66, 114, 117
family members, 17, 18, 22, 23, 43, 50, 58, 59, 64, 87, 95, 111, 113, 118, 120, 141
family planning, 28
family support, 37
farmers, 110
farms, 11, 47, 67
fears, 7, 16
feelings, 19, 51, 65, 89, 90, 94, 113, 118, 145, 150
fertility, 89
financial support, 6, 69, 89
fishing, 26
flexibility, 41, 67, 113, 145
fluid, 63
focus groups, 52
full employment, 2, 79, 130
funding, xii, 66, 98

G

gate-keeping, 10, 125, 126
general education, 30
general practitioner, 97
genes, 65
gestures, 45, 139, 142
God, 55, 59, 96
grades, 71
guidance, 30, 65
guidelines, 168

H

harvesting, 100
health care system, 165
health problems, 89, 127
health services, 12, 22, 27, 28, 40, 41, 58, 75, 80, 97, 116, 134, 164
hearing impairment, 99
hegemony, 148
height, 2, 93, 114
helplessness, 109
hermeneutics, 45, 139, 141
homework, 66, 71, 110
human actions, 143
human rights, 2, 37, 56, 74, 104, 115, 131
human subjects, 146
humanistic perspective, 157
husband, v, 5, 6, 8, 61, 69, 76, 77, 86, 87, 89, 90, 91, 92, 93, 96, 105, 110, 119, 122, 152, 153

I

ice, 72, 95
ideology, 56, 76, 123, 129
idiosyncratic, 129
image, 120
images, 19
imbalances, 146
immunity, 146
immunization, 28
impacts, 14, 15, 128
impairments, 29, 36, 76, 83, 147
independence, 7, 26

Independence, 69
individual rights, 158
inequality, 141
infant mortality, 28
informed consent, 145
inmates, 5, 29, 48, 56, 76
institutionalisation, 39
integration, 30, 56, 58, 70, 74, 75, 78, 167
intellectual disabilities, 36
intelligence, 81
interest groups, 36, 56
intervention, 55, 64
intestine, 85
invasion of privacy, 146
IQ scores, 30
isolation, 58, 109

J

justification, 143

L

labour force, 58, 130
labour market, 34
learners, 30, 31, 70, 72
learning, 2, 6, 9, 10, 31, 32, 70, 71, 99, 106, 107, 114, 123, 125, 144, 159, 166
learning task, 107
legislation, 4, 12, 15, 27, 31, 33, 34, 36, 37, 38, 39, 40, 43, 48, 56, 57, 66, 69, 71, 73, 74, 78, 98, 112, 134
life expectancy, 94, 99
lifestyle changes, 103
lobbying, 105
local authorities, 23, 41, 76
local community, 32
locus, 130
loneliness, 4, 7, 109, 119
longevity, 28
lying, 87, 143

M

majority, 120
management, 22
manual workers, 111

marginalization, 141
marital status, 51, 151
marriage, 48, 66, 79, 85, 93, 111, 112, 115, 153
married couples, 16
medication, 64, 86
medicines, 29
membership, 111, 127, 129
memory, 61, 152
mental health, 98
mental illness, 36, 39
mental retardation, 5, 39, 77, 98, 99, 134
messages, 12
metaphor, 20, 144
methodology, 3, 45, 161
middle class, 10, 70, 127
migrant workers, 110
Ministry of Education, 25, 31, 32, 33, 36, 105, 134, 165
minority groups, 139, 144
mobile phone, 12
mortality rate, 28
multidimensional, 18
murder, 85, 93
muscular dystrophy, 82
music, 5, 151
mutuality, 127

N

narratives, 1, 16, 17, 58, 84, 111, 119, 125, 129, 148, 150
nationality, 38
negative experiences, 101
neglect, 99, 131
negotiating, 59, 80
neurologist, 7, 82, 84, 102
Norway, 31, 168
nuclear family, 17, 18
nurses, 11, 28
nursing, 27, 28
nursing care, 28
nursing home, 27, 28

Index

O

obstacles, 108, 125, 126
old age, 38
opportunities, 8, 24, 36, 51, 70, 105, 162, 165
optimism, 2, 8, 10
osteoporosis, 67

P

pain, 91, 103, 148, 152
parenthood, 68, 168
parenting, 3, 53
participant observation, 141
pensioners, 27, 28
performance, 89
permission, 45, 50, 96, 151
personal history, 141
personal life, 118
persons with disabilities, 97, 157, 164, 165, 167
phenomenology, 45, 139, 141
photographs, 108
policy makers, xi, 4, 130, 142, 154
policy-makers, 76
political leaders, 57
political parties, 124
political party, 112, 127
politics, 25, 112, 144, 155, 165
positive attitudes, 107
poststructuralism, 18
poverty, 27, 30, 130
power relations, 20, 148
pregnancy, 11, 28, 59, 81, 83, 85, 89, 90, 93, 96, 161, 163
prejudice, 47, 149
preschool, 8, 9, 13, 31, 32, 41, 65, 66, 68, 70, 71, 95, 97, 101, 105, 106, 110, 114, 118, 125, 134, 148
preschool children, 134
preschoolers, 32
prevention, 145
problem children, 30
professionalism, 157, 158
prognosis, 42, 84, 90, 151
project, 3, 45, 147
psychologist, 12, 50, 64, 94, 113
psychology, 26, 46, 78, 162
public discourse, 58
public health, 23, 27, 38
public opinion, 56
public policy, 19
public service, 38, 78, 112

Q

qualitative research, 52, 140, 141, 144, 145, 146, 154, 155, 162, 167
quality control, 37
quality of life, 3, 22, 24, 36, 37, 78, 95, 115

R

reactions, x, 4, 18, 118
reading, 26, 39, 52, 61, 101, 153
reality, 19, 45, 63, 157
recommendations, iv
reconstruction, 120
rehabilitation, 9, 27, 28, 76, 125
relatives, 73, 92, 96, 97, 100, 113, 120, 124
relevance, 147
religious beliefs, 94
repression, 128
reputation, 146
resilience, 7, 109, 129
resistance, 10, 70, 105, 147
resource management, 22
resources, 2, 22, 59, 79, 80, 87, 99, 105, 108, 123, 128, 131, 154
restructuring, 25, 34, 98
retardation, 5, 39, 77, 98, 99, 134
rights, 2, 3, 6, 8, 10, 15, 25, 34, 36, 37, 40, 41, 56, 58, 74, 75, 78, 101, 102, 104, 115, 129, 131, 158, 167
role conflict, 148
routines, 9, 17, 59, 118, 119
rural areas, 26, 57, 58, 73, 79, 111, 121

S

Scandinavia, 130

school activities, 146
school community, 106
school psychology, 78
schooling, 5, 30, 42, 49, 51, 55, 66, 69, 70, 75, 80, 86, 94, 97, 105, 106, 107, 108, 125, 134, 151
scientific knowledge, 8
screening, 87, 89, 90, 93, 161
secondary education, 33
secondary schools, 33, 72, 105, 107, 134, 149
selective mutism, 66
self-esteem, 64
self-image, 120
semi-structured interviews, 142
serum, 29
sex, 115
sexual orientation, 47
shame, 69
shape, 17, 74, 98, 153
shock, 61, 64, 102
shyness, 120
sibling, 17, 58, 95, 114, 117, 118, 122
siblings, 7, 105, 118, 147
signs, 5, 31, 64
skimming, 26
small firms, 110
social acceptance, 2
social capital, iv, x, 1, 4, 15, 18, 19, 57, 58, 72, 87, 90, 92, 104, 111, 115, 121, 123, 126, 127, 128, 146, 166
social construct, vii, 18, 19, 20, 22, 25, 45, 147, 157, 161
social influence, 124
social institutions, 20
social justice, 2, 107, 142, 165
social life, 144
social network, 10, 14, 18, 20, 147
social policy, iv, xi, 1, 4, 14, 15, 20, 21, 23, 25, 48, 109, 115, 117, 127, 128, 140, 147
social problems, 30
social relations, 20
social roles, 116
social security, 4, 27, 38, 134, 160, 164, 167
Social Security, viii, 27, 28, 34, 35, 38, 42, 134, 160
social services, 3, 23, 26, 36, 40, 41, 46, 89, 147, 164
social situations, 4, 123
social status, 10, 123, 127
social support, 27
social theory, 159
social workers, 43, 100, 102
solidarity, 110, 147
Spain, 77, 167
special education, 8, 26, 30, 31, 32, 33, 37, 78, 105, 107, 134, 146, 155, 159, 161, 166, 167
specialisation, 28, 62, 98
specialists, 28, 39, 91, 97, 102, 129
specialization, 21, 129
speech, 7, 58, 157
sperm, 16
SSI, viii, ix, x, 9, 27, 28, 35, 38, 39, 40, 43, 62, 67, 68, 69, 79, 102, 103, 104, 111, 127, 134
standard of living, 57, 129
statistics, 79, 82, 97, 165
stigma, 27
stomach, 51, 91
student teacher, 141
subjectivity, 19
substance abuse, 28
supervision, 35, 39
support services, 36, 55, 134
syndrome, 3, 5, 11, 12, 14, 16, 48, 49, 70, 80, 83, 85, 89, 92, 93, 94, 99, 101, 111, 113, 149, 151

T

talent, 114
technological change, 4
teenage girls, 92
teens, 5, 100, 106
terminal illness, 84
therapy, 26, 58, 72
thoughts, 9, 94, 113
tissue, 150, 152
traditions, 143

training, 2, 9, 12, 13, 26, 29, 30, 39, 56, 118
transcripts, 51, 150
transference, 134
transformation, 49
translation, 77
treaties, 34
triangulation, ix
trustworthiness, 52, 130

U

UK, xii
ultrasound, 11, 28, 81, 83, 84, 85, 87, 89, 90, 93, 134
ultrasound screening, 89, 93
UN, 34
UNESCO, 34
United Nations, 34, 75, 167
universities, 2, 31, 149
university education, 72, 93, 124
urban area, 14, 28, 30, 47, 49, 69, 70, 79, 85, 105, 115
urban areas, 14, 28, 30, 47, 49, 69, 70, 79, 115

V

vasectomy, 100

venue, 154
vested interests, 143
vulnerable people, 131

W

walking, 5, 37, 114, 144
wear, 58
web, 3, 53
welfare, ix, x, 1, 2, 3, 6, 22, 25, 26, 27, 37, 38, 48, 49, 53, 129, 130, 147, 158, 165
welfare state, ix, x, 3, 6, 48, 49, 129, 130, 147, 158
welfare system, 1, 2, 27, 130
windows, 8
workers, 2, 29, 43, 59, 62, 77, 79, 84, 100, 102, 110, 111, 141
working hours, 114

Y

young adults, 19

Z

zeitgeist, 96